This essential book demystifies the voyage to becoming a leadership coaching psychologist and should be mandatory reading as part of all coach training programs. More important, adherence to the principles and practices outlined in this book by coaching practitioners will ensure that the leaders they serve will be able to navigate the turbulent seas of today's organizational environments.

—**Krister Lowe, PhD,** Social-Organizational Psychologist, Founder, The Team Coaching Zone, Mount Laurel, NJ, United States

Vicki Vandaveer and Michael Frisch have coauthored an outstanding book on applied coaching psychology and its application to the development of leaders in organizations. This book will be of great interest to both trainees and qualified psychologists who wish to gain an in-depth understanding of this exciting field.

—**Stephen Palmer, PhD,** Professor of Practice, University of Wales Trinity Saint David, Carmarthen, Wales; Fellow of the International Society for Coaching Psychology

Vandaveer and Frisch, two highly experienced consulting psychologists, have captured the essence of leadership coaching. Anyone who is starting on an executive coaching journey or wants to know what is needed to advance their skills as a trusted advisor should read this book with a marker in hand to highlight the wisdom and actions that will add value to their practice.

—**John R. Fulkerson, PhD,** Fulkerson Consulting, New York, NY, United States; Fellow of the American Psychological Association

Vicki Vandaveer and Michael Frisch have made an exceptional contribution to the field of psychology and coaching psychology. They provide a comprehensive understanding of the underlying psychology, applied coaching practices, and supporting research related to leader coaching, and they share their advanced insights and deep professional expertise. The authors have long been central thought leaders and leading practitioners of coaching psychology. This book is a rare opportunity to learn how two extraordinary professional psychologists practice leader coaching.

—**Rob Silzer, PhD,** Managing Director, HR Assessment and Development, Inc.; Industrial-Organizational Psychology Doctoral Faculty, Graduate School, City University of New York, New York, NY, United States

Coaching
Psychology

Fundamentals of Consulting Psychology Book Series

APA FUNDAMENTALS OF CONSULTING PSYCHOLOGY

Coaching Psychology

CATALYZING EXCELLENCE IN ORGANIZATIONAL LEADERSHIP

VICKI V. VANDAVEER AND MICHAEL H. FRISCH

AMERICAN PSYCHOLOGICAL ASSOCIATION

The opinions and statements published are the responsibility of the authors, and such opinions and statements do not necessarily represent the policies of the American Psychological Association.

Published by
American Psychological Association
750 First Street, NE
Washington, DC 20002
https://www.apa.org

Order Department
https://www.apa.org/pubs/books
order@apa.org

In the U.K., Europe, Africa, and the Middle East, copies may be ordered from Eurospan
https://www.eurospanbookstore.com/apa
info@eurospangroup.com

Typeset in Minion by Circle Graphics, Inc., Reisterstown, MD

Printer: Gasch Printing, Odenton, MD
Cover Designer: Naylor Design, Washington, DC

Library of Congress Cataloging-in-Publication Data

Names: Vandaveer, Vicki V., author. | Frisch, Michael H., author.
Title: Coaching psychology : catalyzing excellence in organizational
  leadership / by Vicki V. Vandaveer and Michael H. Frisch.
Description: Washington, DC : American Psychological Association, [2022] |
  Series: Fundamentals of consulting psychology | Includes bibliographical
  references and index.
Identifiers: LCCN 2021055823 (print) | LCCN 2021055824 (ebook) |
  ISBN 9781433840074 (paperback) | ISBN 9781433840081 (ebook)
Subjects: LCSH: Personal coaching. | Executive coaching.
Classification: LCC BF637.P36 V36 2022 (print) | LCC BF637.P36 (ebook) |
  DDC 158.3--dc23/eng/20211129
LC record available at https://lccn.loc.gov/2021055823
LC ebook record available at https://lccn.loc.gov/2021055824

https://doi.org/10.1037/0000293-000

Printed in the United States of America

10 9 8 7 6 5 4 3 2 1

In grateful and loving memory of P. R. "Dick" Jeanneret
and Robert J. "Bob" Lee, luminaries in industrial
and organizational consulting psychology and particularly
in executive assessment and coaching and to whom we are forever
grateful for their mentoring, encouragement, and support.

Contents

Series Editor's Foreword

Rodney L. Lowman

The field of consulting psychology has blossomed in recent years. It covers the applications of psychology in consulting to individuals, teams, organizations, and systems. Unfortunately, there are very few graduate training programs in this field of specialization, so consulting psychology roles are mostly populated by those who came to consulting psychology after having trained in other areas psychology—including industrial and organizational (I/O), clinical/counseling, and school psychology, among others. Yet such training is rarely focused on consulting psychology and psychologists and graduate students therefore have to learn the needed skills through on-the-job training, reading books and articles, attending conferences and workshops, and being mentored in the foundational competencies of the field as they seek to transition into it.

After a number of years of editing *Consulting Psychology Journal: Practice and Research*, the field's flagship journal, I felt that an additional type of educational product was needed to help those transitioning into consulting psychology. The Society of Consulting Psychology therefore partnered with the American Psychological Association to develop a new book series. The idea was to create a series of monographs on specific foundational skill sets needed to practice in this area of specialization. Working with an editorial Advisory Board, consisting of Drs. Judith Blanton, Brodie Gregory, Skipton Leonard (and initially Dale Fuqua and the late Edward Pavur, Jr.) and myself, our goal in the series has been to identify the major competencies needed by consulting psychologists and then to work with highly experienced authors to create short, accessible, evidence-based texts that would be useful both as stand-alone volumes and in combination with one another. The readers would be graduate students in relevant training programs, psychologists planning a transition into consulting psychology, and practicing professionals who want to add to their areas of expertise.

What are the fundamental skills needed in consulting psychology practice? The following sources provide useful starting points:

■ *Guidelines for Education and Training at the Doctoral and Post-doctoral Level in Consulting Psychology (CP)/Organizational Consulting Psychology (OCP)*, created by the Society of Consulting Psychology, and approved by the American Psychological Association in 2017 (Gullette et al., 2019)
■ *Handbook of Organizational Consulting Psychology* (Lowman, 2002)
■ *An Introduction to Consulting Psychology: Working With Individuals, Groups, and Organizations* (Lowman, 2016a)

Each of these contributions was organized around the concept of levels (individual, group, and organizational) as a taxonomy for identifying fundamental skills. Within and across each of those categories, two broad skill sets are needed: assessment and intervention.

As with many areas of psychological practice, the foundational skills that apply in one area may overlap into others in the taxonomy. Interventions with individuals, as in executive coaching, for instance, usually take place in the context of work with a specific team and within specific organizations, which themselves also constitute a type of "client" (Schein, 1999). Understanding the systemwide issues and dynamics at the organizational level usually also involves consulting activities with specific executives and teams, and multicultural/international issues suffuse many of our roles. The APA Guidelines and the *Handbook* concluded, properly, that consulting psychologists need to be trained in and have, at least, foundational skills and experience at the individual, group, and organizational levels, even if they primarily specialize in one of these areas.

In inviting you to learn more about consulting psychology through this book series, I hope you will come to agree that this is an exciting and inherently interesting area of study, research, and professional practice. The series aims not just to cover relevant literature on specific topics in consulting psychology but also to capture the richness of this work by including case material that illustrates its applications. Readers will soon understand that consulting psychologists are real-world activists, energized by the opportunity to work in, and to have positive impact on, real-world environments.

Finally, as one who trained and practiced in both I/O and clinical psychology, I should note that consulting psychology has been the one area in which I felt that all of my training and skill sets were both welcomed and needed. And in a world where organizations and the individuals and teams within them greatly need help in functioning ethically and effectively, in bridging individual, group, and organization-level needs and constituencies, and in coping with the rapid expansion of knowledge and escalating competition and internationalization, this book series aims to make a difference by helping more psychologists join the ranks of qualified consulting psychologists. Collectively, we can have positive impact not just on an area of specialization in psychology, but also the world.

ABOUT THIS BOOK

My areas of professional practice in consulting psychology included "coaching" long before coaching became the burgeoning area of practice that it now is. Today there is a large and ever-expanding army of coaches eager to provide their services to managers, executives, and others. Many of these people are well-trained professionals, but others are not. Indeed, there are currently few barriers to offering one's services as a professional coach. Yet, for consulting psychologists, coaching is just one of a number of fundamental skills needed to do their work effectively (see Gullette et al., 2019; Lowman, 2016a).

Vicki Vandaveer and Michael Frisch, the authors of this book, were also coaching psychologists (CPs) long before the field became fashionable. Each of them has had many years of experience applying their psychological expertise to consulting with individuals, teams, and organizations. Their approach to coaching exemplifies what their book advocates. It integrates individual dynamics with those found in the groups and organizations in which they were embedded. But it does much more than that. It shows how coaching psychology is different from—and how it overlaps—other approaches to coaching. The book argues for the need to determine the effectiveness of coaching efforts and also immerses its readers in the considerable number of ethical issues that can arise in doing this work.

This is not just another book on coaching. Rather, it shows how CPs and those eager to move in that direction can and should make use of psychological knowledge and expertise to practice coaching that is both evidence- and experience-based. Although the book is written with psychologists and graduate psychology students in mind, it can also be read and made use of by nonpsychologist coaches and those in training to become coaches. Both authors have published in this area (e.g., Frisch et al., 2012; Vandaveer, 2012a; Vandaveer et al., 2016) and are knowledgeable about the coaching research literature. But it is the depth and breadth of their professional practice experience in applying coaching psychology that make this book truly distinctive and an excellent introduction to coaching psychology.

Preface

Individual coaching for the professional development of leaders has become a well-established key component of overall leader development in organizations worldwide. This significant and continuously increasing demand for coaching over the past 30 years has drawn thousands of people from a variety of backgrounds to this field, and the field itself has morphed and changed as a result.

As part of the *Fundamentals of Consulting Psychology* book series, this book is intended as a foundational guide for those with advanced training in psychology who want to learn about coaching in organizational contexts and possibly begin the process of adding this practice area to their professional activities. If you are currently a psychologist—in any area of psychology—or a graduate student in psychology, this book is written to help you decide whether—and how—to prepare to become a coaching psychologist (CP). We hope this book also will be helpful to all others who do executive and leader coaching.

CPs help individuals learn, grow, excel, and realize their potential in the contexts in which they work. Coaching is a helping professional activity; CPs help individuals learn and grow by facilitating learning, discovery, breakthrough insights, and skill-building and by identifying their sources of personal and professional excellence in organizational roles.

Psychologists and psychology graduate students have much to offer the practice of leader coaching. Regardless of which area of psychology one's advanced degree is (or will be) in, no one emerges from graduate school or other practice areas of psychology fully prepared to coach leaders. Coaching psychology is distinctly different from therapy, counseling, or organization development, yet it draws from those areas of psychology, as well as from the evidence bases of social, developmental, and cognitive psychology and cognitive neuroscience—and other areas and disciplines (e.g., management, social anthropology). All areas of psychology offer a valuable perspective from which to view and understand organizational leader development and effectiveness, but any one area must be supplemented with knowledge and skill proficiency in other areas to be effective in coaching leaders within the contexts in which they work (Vandaveer et al., 2016).

My (VV's) path to executive coaching originated with doctoral training in an industrial and organizational (I/O) psychology program that emphasized the quantitative research side of I/O psychology, job analysis, psychometrics, test development and validation, and applied organizational research—supported by the primary theories of social and social-organizational, cognitive, leadership, organization development, and motivation psychology and psychometrics. Transitioning from predicting an individual's effectiveness in a leadership role to helping individuals excel as leaders has been challenging, interesting, and immensely professionally and personally fulfilling. I describe executive and leader coaching psychology as being in the "sweet spot" of the intersection of my interests, abilities and skills, values, and motivational drivers. Might this area of professional practice be the same for you? (Note that there is a more detailed description of my path from I/O psychology to coaching psychology in Chapter 5.)

My (MF's) path to coaching also was anchored in I/O psychology (we met while interning at the same consulting firm but studying in different doctoral programs) but expanded as organizational practices in the 1980s included more interventions at the level of the individual (e.g., 360-degree feedback, leader competencies, individual development planning) that required a one-to-one helping relationship not taught in traditional I/O psychology programs. Drawing on sensibilities initiated in early home life (clinical psychology was the family business) and then adding formal postdoctoral therapist training resulted in a combination of knowledge and skills conducive to executive coaching. As luck would have it, the mixing of these elements coincided with the zeitgeist of coaching, yielding a gratifying career delivering many types of coaching services to organizations, training new coaches, supervising experienced coaches, and reflecting and writing about all those challenges.

We hope you will benefit from the information in this introductory book on coaching psychology. We have strived to provide a realistic preview of the work of coaching organizational leaders, as well as guidance in what you can do to best prepare for becoming a CP if you feel a strong attraction to this work, as we do.

For those of you who do not have an advanced degree in psychology, we welcome you as well to this *Fundamentals of Consulting Psychology* book, and if you share our passion for helping leaders and their organizations become the best they can be, we hope that you too will be interested in preparing yourself to become a CP.

Acknowledgments

I acknowledge with deep gratitude the following individuals who have been role models, mentors, thought partners, encouragers, and gentle nudgers in my learning journey to build expertise in coaching psychology: John Carter, John Fulkerson, Pamela Kennedy-Stinson, Dick Kilburg, Rodney Lowman, Alok Sawhney, Rob Silzer, Karol Wasylyshyn, my Society of Consulting Psychology peer consultation colleagues, International Society for Coaching Psychology colleagues, and my executive clients over many years. I'm especially grateful to my family for their constant support and encouragement for my professional pursuits: Betty, Noel, Melanie, Jeanie, Bobby.

—Vicki V. Vandaveer

I would like to acknowledge my coaching students and alumni of the iCoachNY Professional Coaching Program at Baruch College, my teaching colleagues Karen Metzger, Donna Marcus, and Jeremy Robinson and our organizational sponsors. As the saying goes, teaching is learning, and many, if not all, of my ideas about becoming an executive coach were born and evolved in the crucible of creating practical and inspiring content and pedagogy. I would also like to acknowledge my growing family's constant interest in and support for my writing efforts.

—Michael H. Frisch

Coaching
Psychology

Introduction

Coaching psychology is an area of general applied psychology that brings psychological principles and methods to the professional practice of coaching organizational leaders. Its purposes are to help individuals and teams (a) elevate their performance and effectiveness as leaders, (b) develop required skills for advancing into leadership roles in organizations, and/or (c) prepare for transitions into different leader roles (e.g., higher level or international assignment) using evidence-based methods grounded in scientific research.

While coaching psychology is also used in many different settings (e.g., sports, life, teams), the focus of this book, as part of the American Psychological Association (APA) *Fundamentals of Consulting Psychology* book series, is developmental coaching of leaders in organizations.

https://doi.org/10.1037/0000293-001

Coaching Psychology: Catalyzing Excellence in Organizational Leadership, by V. V. Vandaveer and M. H. Frisch

Consider the following example of a 6-month coaching engagement with Leo, a department manager with the Apex Corporation:

> Leo had advanced quickly in management roles and now had a full department reporting to him and had much-increased exposure to senior management. He and his manager had openly talked about several areas for growth, including empowering his team members more fully so he could focus on bigger picture items and "polishing" his skill in communicating with senior leaders in the organization (referring to his executive presence). A 6-month executive coaching engagement was planned to help Leo elevate his effectiveness in these two areas. Leo engaged quickly with his coach, Rick. As part of getting to know Leo and to better understand the specific behaviors related to the two identified development areas, Rick asked Leo to complete a standardized leadership assessment inventory, and Rick conducted confidential feedback interviews with Leo's manager, direct reports, selected peers, and senior leaders. The information from these assessments helped them fine-tune Leo's development goals. They prepared a draft development action plan highlighting Leo's leadership strengths and the focus areas for development, noting how progress for each goal would be measured. That plan was the basis of a robust four-way conversation with Leo, Rick, Leo's manager, and his human resources (HR) business partner. The resulting approved development plan provided the foundation for Leo's and Rick's coaching over the next 5 months. At the end of the coaching engagement, Leo, Rick, Leo's manager, and his HR business partner reconvened, noting the good progress accomplished; they set the stage for Leo's continued development, mentored by his manager, with follow-up check-ins with the HR business partner.

Often, individual coaching is part of an overall program for leader development, usually preceded by leadership training, and sometimes it is an integral part of more multifaceted training and development programs. Many organizations send their high-potential employees to executive education programs in university-based schools of business, such as Stanford; Michigan; Wharton; Columbia; Chicago Booth; Washington–Olin; Harvard; Massachusetts Institute of Technology; North Carolina;

Chicago; Northwestern; University of California, Berkeley; Yale; and Duke (these U.S. schools are taken from 2019 and 2020 rankings of best executive education programs in the *Financial Times*). There is tremendous value in these programs, not the least of which is the opportunity for participants to meet and interact with leaders like themselves from many different organizations.

There is a point, however, at which more formal classroom training does not significantly increase an individual's effectiveness, and further development that is more individualized has been found to help many leaders continue to learn and become more effective leaders. It's a little like hiking up a mountain and getting to the "false summit"—which is a real achievement, and it's fine to declare success at that point. To get to the very top, however, the trail typically gets narrower, steeper, and more challenging, with success depending on personal attributes such as relevant knowledge and skills, motivation, courage, sometimes pure grit (i.e., perseverance, fortitude, tenacity), and not infrequently, innovativeness. Success also depends on understanding one's own strengths and limitations, and in addition, it requires making the most of the former and managing the latter well—for instance, drawing on the strengths and skills of team members (S. D. Axelrod, 2005). The postscript is this: Getting to the very top of the mountain is exhilarating, but once a person gets there, it's clear that there is yet a higher top. There always seems to be a greater challenge to achieve, including continually gaining more effectiveness as a leader.

Most leaders we have worked with believe that they can always get better—no matter what their aspirations and how effective they are now. These are the people for whom individualized coaching is best suited. Coaching helps leaders identify what they are made of by taking a good look at themselves, often discovering talents and capabilities that they were not fully aware of, better understanding their limitations, and gaining insight into their impact on others and the organization. Organizations that invest in executive development coaching as a perk for high-potential leaders also may use coaching to help an individual improve in one or two areas to have the best chance to be considered as high potential and be placed on leader succession lists. Leader development is about discovery and learning: learning how to leverage talents, build skills, and effectively manage weaknesses for even greater effectiveness in leadership roles. It is also about getting off to the best possible start in a new role. And for many, it is about self-actualization: developing to one's full potential (Maslow, 1943).

Thus, most leader and executive coaching by psychologists is for leaders who (a) are already effective and wish to advance to the next levels of effectiveness, (b) are considered to have the potential for succession to higher levels of leadership, or (c) need to refine some aspects of their leadership to become even more effective in their current role or to be considered ready for advancement.

Occasionally, coaching is also used by some organizations to help individuals turn around substandard performance or problematic behaviors. Typically, such an investment in coaching is for individuals who are valuable to the organization except for one or more behaviors that detract from overall effectiveness and that both the individual and management believe can be changed.

DEFINITION OF COACHING PSYCHOLOGY

Coaching psychology is a subset of organizational consulting psychology—that is, coaching is organizational consulting at the individual level (Kilburg & Diedrich, 2007; Lowman, 2002, 2016a, 2016b). Our working definition is the following:

> Coaching psychology is an evidence-based, experience-driven individualized process of professional development in which a psychologist works one-to-one with individuals in their organizational contexts to help them prepare for and enhance their effectiveness in organizational roles. (See Vandaveer et al., 2016, p. 127, for the research definition from which this one is derived.)

Thus, our definition of a coaching psychologist (CP) is anyone with an advanced degree in psychology (any area) who is using knowledge of and expertise in psychology as a foundation for coaching leaders. That foundation of advanced level training in the science of human behavior and cognition is invaluable to the professional practice of executive coaching, supplemented by postgrad degree training in other areas (see Chapter 5). Notice the key term *help* in the definition. CPs help individuals "unlock their potential to maximize their own performance" (Whitmore, 2017, pp. 12–13). Sir John Whitmore likened coaching for leader development to Timothy Gallwey's (1997) concept of coaching great tennis players in *The Inner Game of Tennis*—the formula for which is P = p – i (Performance = potential minus interference).

Fundamentally, coaching leaders—as in coaching athletes, musicians, others—is about facilitating individuals' learning by minimizing or eliminating their internal "interferences" to fulfill their potential, which manifests in elevated performance and effectiveness as a leader. That is, coaching is all about the "inner game."

BACKGROUND AND HISTORY OF COACHING PSYCHOLOGY

Coaching by psychologists in the United States has deep roots, dating back to the 1940s (Gebhardt, 2016; Hart et al., 2001; Kilburg, 2016). As a part of organizational consulting (Lowman, 2002, 2016a, 2016b), one-on-one executive development work was referred to as, among other things, *management consulting* or *executive consulting, individual executive development*, and *advising*, and it was not called *executive coaching* until the 1980s (Manuso, 1983).

Pioneered by psychologist practitioners, coaching psychology as an area of professional practice has had the underpinnings of scientific theories and frameworks from a wide range of psychological practice areas, although, naturally, the CP's area of graduate training has the greatest influence on what that person primarily draws from (e.g., clinical, counseling, industrial and organizational, social psychology, developmental, and/or cognitive; Vandaveer et al., 2016). More recently, a strong foundation of science and research for the practice of coaching psychology has been emerging (Athanasopoulou & Dopson, 2018; Baron & Morin, 2010; Boyatzis & Jack, 2018; Cavanagh et al., 2005; de Haan et al., 2013, 2016, 2019, 2020; De Meuse et al., 2009; Dixit & Dixit, 2018; Grant, 2013; Grant et al., 2010; Graßmann et al., 2020; Grover & Furnham, 2016; Jones et al., 2016; Lane & Corrie, 2009; Laske, 2007; Moen & Skaalvik, 2009; Nowack & Mashihi, 2012; Page & de Haan, 2014; Peterson, 2010; Steinbrenner & Schlosser, 2011; Theeboom et al., 2013; Vandaveer et al., 2016; Van Oosten et al., 2019; Wasylyshyn, 2003; Williams & Lowman, 2018).

For a comprehensive review of coaching internationally, see Cox et al. (2014), Grant et al. (2010), Palmer and Whybrow (2008), and the professional journal *International Coaching Psychology Review* published by the British Psychology Society (https://www.bps.org.uk/publications/international-coaching-psychology-review).

At this writing, there is a patchwork of models and standards for coaching practice, and there are few barriers to entry. Many psychologists and health services providers who are not trained in coaching but wish to begin offering coaching services often do not seek retraining because they are unaware of the considerable differences between coaching and clinical or counseling psychology (Gebhardt, 2016; Hart et al., 2001). We have encountered a few organizations in which executive coaching is seen as executive psychotherapy, which serves to confuse potential clients of both types of services and which, in some cases, has served to tarnish the regard for coaching in business settings because psychological therapy often means "mental illness" to the layperson. We hope that this book serves to differentiate coaching by psychologists from other services they may offer; highlight unique aspects, challenges, and satisfaction of coaching leaders; and provide specific steps that psychologists can take to move toward delivering coaching services within organizational contexts.

BOOK OVERVIEW

In Chapter 1, having defined and described coaching psychology, we examine how it is the same as and different from other types of psychologists' work with individuals to help them have a better life (i.e., therapy, counseling, mentoring), including the primary theoretical and scientific evidence bases supporting each method. Then the reader gets "the lay of the land," a comprehensive overview of coaching psychology, beginning with "who are the clients"—different types and roles, levels of coaching complexity and associated types of coaching expertise needed at each level, and a case vignette to illustrate key points.

Chapter 2 begins with a high-level overview of the coaching engagement, from initial contact to contracting to managing the coaching engagement to the process of coaching to development planning to concluding the engagement and evaluating the results. Then, aided by a visual of the coaching engagement, the reader is guided through the process in some detail from beginning to conclusion, emphasizing effective management of the engagement as well as the coaching process itself. Common pitfalls are also described, along with tips on how to avoid them—and/or how to address them if they occur.

The focus of Chapter 3 is on the coaching process itself, including a description of many of the "tools" that help facilitate the client's learning. A description of the important preparation of the CP's self is followed by detailed descriptions of the primary methods, models, theoretical frameworks, and practical learning aids involved in coaching psychology. The references cited are rich sources of information and perspectives, and we encourage the reader to dive into them in particular areas of their interest.

An organization's investment in individualized leader coaching is significant. So, how effective is coaching? How can we know? Coaching effectiveness is difficult to measure for a variety of reasons articulated in Chapter 4. This chapter summarizes the main research to date and their outcomes and also suggests to CPs what they can do to know how effective their coaching is and what they can do to continually improve.

As illustrated by both our paths to coaching, all professionals seeking to do executive coaching need training beyond graduate school. Choices of which additional training is needed are based on individual background and aspirations (like coaching itself!), but it needs to be a reasoned and informed decision. Chapter 5 walks readers through a menu of options for preparing to offer coaching services.

All professional services provided to people require a thorough knowledge of and adherence to established ethical principles and standards of one's profession. Psychology has a long tradition of considering and articulating ethical standards for professional practice. Chapter 6 refers to the APA (2017) *Ethical Principles of Psychologists and Code of Conduct* and its application to coaching in organizational contexts. We provide several case vignettes as examples.

The case vignettes presented to illustrate key points are all composites of actual coaching cases we have had. None are from the work of a single client or company, and individuals' names are fictitious to protect anonymity. The situations, however, are real.

We recognize that there are many more nonpsychologists than psychologists who do coaching, and we hope that all coaches will find useful information in this book. We also hope that some readers will decide to pursue advanced training in the science and practice of psychology to further enrich their knowledge of individual and social psychology of leadership dynamics in organizations as a basis for their coaching.

In this introduction, we have provided an overview of this book, including our operating definition of "coaching psychology" and a high-level review of the history of coaching within the larger professional practice area of consulting psychology. With this framework in place, Chapter 1 takes a closer look at coaching psychology, including comparisons with clinical and counseling psychology and mentoring.

1

Coaching Psychology: Individualized Leader Development

This chapter compares coaching psychology with psychotherapy, counseling, and mentoring—first describing each area, then comparing coaching psychology with each of the other areas. Next, we consider who a coaching psychologist's (CP's) clients are (there are almost always more than one), and we wrap up with a description of the levels of complexity of coaching engagements and what coaching psychology looks like for each.

COACHING PSYCHOLOGY

The practice of leadership coaching psychology has roots in and draws from many areas of psychology, including clinical, counseling, industrial and organizational, developmental, social, cross-cultural, gestalt,

https://doi.org/10.1037/0000293-002
Coaching Psychology: Catalyzing Excellence in Organizational Leadership, by V. V. Vandaveer and M. H. Frisch

and neuropsychology—all applied within the domain of consulting psychology (Lowman, 2002; Williams & Lowman, 2018). Because leadership coaching is a one-to-one helping relationship, clinical and counseling psychology have contributed the most in terms of typology of coaching methods, the principles and ethics of working with individuals (Gebhardt, 2016), associated research methods, and of course, the intuitive and artful elements of working with individuals.

Working with organizational leaders one-to-one to help them develop as maximally effective leaders in their organizational roles and context, the CP focuses on helping individuals to (a) fully recognize and appreciate their strongest leadership related abilities, skills, and personal attributes, fine-tuning and, even better, leveraging them to enhance their effectiveness and desired impact on individuals and the organization; (b) identify key focus areas to strengthen or develop; and, in many cases, (c) create and implement a personalized development plan. The CP and coaching client work together to discover and develop the client's expertise and unique, most effective leadership style, the CP serving as a facilitator of the client's learning and development.

THERAPY AND PSYCHOTHERAPY

The focus of psychotherapy is helping the individual (referred to as the "patient") deal with deep-seated emotional issues and unconscious internal conflicts. "Psychotherapy addresses the deep, unconscious, long-standing personality and behaviour problems and patterns of clients rather than focusing on and superficially resolving only their presenting symptoms" (Feltham & Palmer, 2015, p. 7). Psychotherapy attends to "entrenched psychological distress patterns, usually thought to derive from very early relationships in childhood and/or from partly innate drives . . . and requires a substantial time commitment . . . [potentially] meeting several times a week for several years" (Feltham & Palmer, 2015, p. 7). Depending on the nature and severity of the patient's diagnosed problems, the therapist may use a variety of therapeutic approaches to treatment, ranging from cognitive-behavioral or behavioral approaches to psychoanalysis and psychodynamic therapies to discover (the patient's) unconscious meanings and motivations.

COUNSELING PSYCHOLOGY

Counselling is mostly dedicated to enhancing or restoring clients' own self-understanding, decision-making resources, risk taking and personal growth; and/or helping people with common personal problems such as relationship difficulties, anxiety, depression, stress, life crises, grief, low self-esteem or sense of self efficacy. . . . It is often very short term, usually [meeting] once weekly. (Feltham & Palmer, 2015, p. 6)

It is focused on the presenting issues and how the client (or patient) is thinking about and approaching them. A common approach is the "client-centered, non-directive approach of Carl Rogers . . . [which] rests heavily and optimistically on belief in the innate resourcefulness and goodness of human beings" (Feltham & Palmer, 2015, p. 6; Sharf, 2010).

MENTORING

Mentoring is a more recent aspect of leader development in organizations, although mentoring has existed for thousands of years. According to some, the concept was introduced with the character Mentor in Homer's *Odyssey*. The French poet François Fénelon developed Mentor as a wise character in his 1699 novel *Les Adventures de Télémaque* (Morrish, 2020). Mentoring can be a pivotal learning and development experience for anyone and is particularly valuable for anyone wishing to be an effective leader in their organization, anyone new to an organization, and members of diverse and/or underrepresented groups (W. Axelrod, 2019). Typically, mentors are seasoned leaders, and mentees are early-career professionals or new leaders looking for guidance about career and internal advancement. Mentors and mentees usually meet on a mutually determined frequency to discuss whatever is on the mentee's mind. Examples include career aspirations, how to navigate the power dynamics of the organization, how to tackle a current challenge, how to avoid common pitfalls in pursuing their goals, and so forth. Mentors may share stories from their careers by way of example and provide encouragement. To the extent feasible, mentors may also observe mentees in the normal course of organizational life, providing feedback and suggestions for even greater effectiveness. In summary, mentors serve as valuable sounding boards on a host of issues for the mentee.

HOW DOES COACHING PSYCHOLOGY COMPARE WITH THERAPY, COUNSELING, AND MENTORING?

Similarities

In therapy and counseling, the psychologist works with individuals one-on-one to help them become more effective and achieve their goals and aspirations. For coaching, therapy, and counseling psychology, confidentiality is strictly maintained (potential exceptions are clearly stated up front, such as "duty to warn" in therapy and sharing a development plan in coaching) to enable free discussion of sensitive issues in a safe environment. All typically use a wide variety of methods and tools with varying degrees of structure to help individuals achieve their goals. All these practice areas also hold the same fundamental assumption that by enhancing the individual's effectiveness, the effectiveness of the larger social unit of which they are a member (e.g., organization, team, family) is also improved. And in all these areas, the quality of the relationship between the helper/facilitator and the coaching client/patient is a critically important success factor.

Coaching psychology, psychotherapy, and counseling are all supported by the rich evidence bases of psychology—the science of human behavior and cognition (i.e., what individuals do; what and how they think, process information, and solve problems; what motivates and drives them; what they feel, believe, and need; what they fear). The helping approaches that psychologists from all these areas use are primarily those of their graduate training. However, the most effective psychologists in all these areas use several different theoretical models and frameworks because the more perspectives a coach, counselor, or therapist can use to understand an individual in their context, the more complete is their understanding and the more effective the intervention will likely be (Kauffman & Hodgetts, 2016).

Because coaching psychology is about helping leaders become more effective in their organizational contexts, important theoretical foundations of coaching psychology pertain to the organizational context and include organizational theory, social psychology, leadership, work motivation, personality, social-organizational dynamics, organizational change, psychometric theory, individual assessment, organizational-development methods, and meta-analysis of research studies.

Coaching psychology also draws from developmental psychology for principles of adult learning, stages and characteristics of adult development and maturation. In addition, a good number of CPs, including the first author, incorporate many aspects of Gestalt psychology into their coaching. Gestalt psychology emphasizes the whole person within their context and maintaining awareness of the present and the interaction dynamics of the person within their context; individuals are expected to assume responsibility for themselves. Cognitive neuroscience is a newer significant contributor to the knowledge base of leadership and coaching, addressing the actual cognitive and affective structures and processes in the brain that underlie human behavior, motivation, decision making, and change.

Psychologists who are clinically trained approach leader coaching naturally using their clinical therapeutic lens. In fact, in the Vandaveer et al. (2016) study, 30% of study participants indicated that they use a psychodynamic or psychotherapeutic approach. (See Chapter 3, this volume, page 59, which shows the relative percentages of subject matter experts in that study who indicated using each of the theoretical bases listed; note that instructions were to "check all theories that they apply in their coaching.")

Because the practice of coaching by psychologists preceded research on coaching by many years—and because at this writing there are no graduate programs in coaching psychology in the United States—naturally, psychologists rely on the theoretical areas and evidence bases of their graduate training, supplementing their knowledge and skills by learning from other areas to be well prepared for coaching leaders in organizations. Thus, coaching psychology draws from a wide range of areas of psychology, and the particular theoretical lenses used varies across CPs.

Mentoring also draws on the knowledge base of psychology, primarily social learning theory, often obtained indirectly through leadership training and development. Mentors have often had a professional coach themselves and have been informed by what they have read by psychologists and other organizational behavior and leadership experts—filtered, refined, and honed through years of hands-on experience leading, managing, and successfully performing in leadership roles.

Differences

Coaching Psychology

The differences between coaching psychology and psychotherapy and counseling are in (a) purpose, (b) focus, and (c) context, including the nature of the work.

The purpose of coaching psychology is to enhance an individual leader's performance through improved leadership effectiveness in one's current role or prepare for transitioning into a different lateral or higher level leadership role. Leadership coaching also aims to benefit that leader's group and the organization as a whole.

Coaching psychology focuses on increasing effectiveness in leadership roles and the organization's culture, primarily in the present and at the client's levels of conscious or subconscious awareness such that development-relevant topics and insight can be brought into consciousness. The work is proactive and focused on present and future development rather than remedial performance improvement—although, occasionally, coaching may be used to help an otherwise successful individual change one or more problematic behaviors. Coaching psychology work ranges from leadership skills development to advisory consultation and thought partnership on a wide range of leadership and organizational behavior and performance issues.

Leader development coaching represents a significant investment on the part of the organization; therefore, it is primarily used with individuals being prepared for leadership roles at higher levels, with current leaders who wish to become even more effective in their current role, or, less frequently, with individuals who have valuable knowledge or skills but have one or more problematic behaviors that must improve (remedial coaching).

The CP facilitates the client's learning and development for greater effectiveness in the organizational context that the client experiences, interprets, interacts with, responds to, and in which they seek to be maximally effective as leaders. The context includes everything from the organization's culture (e.g., ranging from "high performance" to "laissez-faire," intense to laid-back, internally cooperative to competitive) to the people the client works with and reports to and the client's relationships with them to the nature of the business and its market and financial standings and everything else that impacts an individual's performance, sense of well-being, sense of self-efficacy, the nature of the challenges in their role, and so on.

Of course, the client's larger "environment," such as home life, family relationships, and so forth, can impact their work as well. Chapter 6 addresses the issue of a coaching client's emotional distress pertaining to causes unrelated to their work.

Therapy

Psychotherapy differs from coaching psychology in the following ways.

The purpose of psychotherapy is to help individuals cope with life's stresses or clinical conditions such as neuroses or psychoses or internal conflicts causing distress.

The focus of psychotherapy is typically on internal unresolved emotional conflicts, delving deeply into unconscious factors and early formative experiences and relationships. As described earlier, "psychotherapy . . . takes very seriously the client's psychopathology, or entrenched psychological distress patterns, usually thought to derive from very early relationships in childhood and/or from partly innate drives" (Feltham & Palmer, 2015, p. 6).

As for the context and nature of the work, health care and mental health–related therapy are typically covered by health insurance. "Psychotherapy requires a substantial time commitment, sometimes demanding that patients attend therapy sessions several times a week for years" but can also include less intensive and brief engagements (Feltham & Palmer, 2015, p. 6).

Counseling

Counseling psychology and psychotherapy are often thought of by lay-people as the same, and in many respects, they are. However, there are differences, beginning with graduate psychology training. The curricula overlap somewhat, but the focus is different, preparing counseling psychologists to help patients as described here (Sharf, 2010).

Unlike coaching psychology, the purpose of counseling psychology is to help people better cope in everyday life. Common presenting problems are stress, anxiety, relationship problems, depression, and the need to be generally more effective in their life (e.g., be more assertive, manage stress, move through grief).

Typically, counseling focuses on the "here and now," helping the patient (or client) deal with their identified problems. Like psychotherapy, counseling is "talk therapy"; however, the focus is on the present and immediate past, usually not delving deeply into childhood relationships. Like coaching psychology, the counseling psychologist facilitates the patient's (client's) learning and problem solving; however, it is not usually focused on the individual's work environment.

Counseling psychology is about mental health and well-being, and fees for service may be paid by health insurance. The length of the counseling engagement is typically shorter than for psychotherapy, and the frequency of meetings is less—typically once a week or biweekly.

It should be noted that occasionally there are coaching clients who experience significant emotional or behavioral challenges that interfere with productivity and leadership effectiveness. For those individuals, the CP should consider making a referral to a counseling or clinical colleague for therapy. Depending on the circumstances, leadership coaching may or may not continue at that time, with the decision made by the client, therapist, and CP—and with the appropriate releases.

Mentoring

Mentoring can be distinguished from coaching psychology in the following ways.

The purpose of mentoring is to enhance the individual's learning and understanding, particularly of the organizational context, including informal, unwritten "rules" and expectations and benefiting careerwise from the wisdom of more senior, accomplished executives (Frisch et al., 2012).

The focus of mentoring is to help individuals enhance their effectiveness in the organization, including helping them effectively navigate the organizational power dynamics as they advance in the leadership hierarchy. The mentor may help the mentee expand their professional network and enhance their career prospects (W. Axelrod, 2019).

Unlike coaching, the mentor gives advice and shares wisdom from the mentor's professional and personal experience and sometimes helps the mentee make connections or even serves as the mentee's advocate for advancement in the organization. Mentoring can be a pivotal learning and development experience—especially for emerging and newer leaders.

The best mentoring relationships involve two-way learning. Senior leaders serving as mentors have much they can learn from those who are earlier in careers and who are therefore members of a younger generation. Differences may exist between mentor and mentee, such as values, family structures, social media, and facility with technology. We regard exposure to these differences as benefiting the mentor as much as the mentee. The reciprocal nature of mentoring is a powerful learning tool that goes a long way to bridging generations, benefiting both participants and their organization.

Mentors who are more senior than their mentees sometimes become organizational sponsors as well, advocating for the mentees and making introductions and helping open doors for them. Having a sponsor is tremendously helpful for anyone who aspires to greater challenges and positions of increasing responsibility and influence.

WHO IS THE CLIENT?

An important issue in coaching psychology is the CP's awareness of who will be affected by their coaching work with an individual—that is, who is the client? (Or who are the clients?) As Lowman (2002) conceptualized in his *Handbook of Organizational Consulting Psychology*, consulting psychology operates at the organizational, group, and individual levels. Coaching is consulting at the individual level. It is important to recognize that whenever we consult with an organization, we have multiple "clients" of whom we always need to be aware. Schein (1999) identified six types of organizational clients:

- The *contact client* is the person who first contacts the CP about a problem or need. In the case of executive coaching, the contact client may be a human resources (HR) or leadership development professional, a line manager, or an executive who wishes to provide a direct report— or themselves—with a leadership coach.
- *Intermediate clients* are the individuals or groups who get involved in various interviews, meetings, and other activities as the project evolves. In coaching, these may include managers, team members, and other key stakeholders.
- The *primary client* is the individual (or individuals) who ultimately own the problem or issue being worked on. Both the *coaching client* and the person who authorizes payment for coaching services, if different, are considered to be primary clients (i.e., typically the coaching client and their manager).
- *Unwitting clients* are members of the organization or client system above, below, and in lateral relationships to the primary clients who will be affected by interventions but who are not aware that they will be impacted. In coaching, these might be the coaching client's internal recipients, users of their work, or other colleagues outside of the work group or business unit.
- The *ultimate clients* are the community, the entire organization, investors and private equity owners, an occupational group, or some other group whose welfare and benefit must be considered, even indirectly, in the intervention.

- *Involved "nonclients"* are members of the organization who are aware of the coaching, who do not fit any of the other client definitions, and whose interests may be to slow down or stop the coaching work.

To Schein's (1999) classification of types of clients, we add *indirect clients*, individuals who are aware of the coaching work and are not in contact with the CP and who may feel either positive or negative about these effects. In coaching, these indirect clients might be the coaching client's extended team or peers if they are not intermediate clients.

It is important to recognize that the work of a CP impacts, directly or indirectly, all these clients in some way. Having multiple "clients" is an important element of the context in which coaching takes place, and it covers, by implication, the breadth and depth of awareness and skills required by CPs.

In the case of Leo, both Leo and his manager are **primary clients**. His manager funds and monitors the coaching process, while Leo is responsible for the positive behavioral change that the process aims to achieve. (Note that in this book, we refer to Leo as the coaching client.) The HR or talent management (TM) representative could be both a **contact** and **intermediate client**; that person often has sourced coaching resources and will be checking in with Leo from time to time to see how he is doing and how his development is going. The people the CP, Rick, interviewed for collecting key stakeholders' perceptions of Leo's top strengths as a leader and an area or two that he might improve are also **intermediate clients**. Leo's direct reports and peer colleagues are **indirect clients** (if they did not participate in the feedback interviews but know that Leo is receiving executive development coaching). Other key stakeholders who will be impacted but are not aware that Leo is receiving coaching are **unwitting clients**. The CP must always be cognizant of the potential effects on each of these types of clients and ensure an effective process and outcomes throughout the coaching engagement. Furthermore, the CP is responsible for ensuring that effective mechanisms are in place at the conclusion of the coaching engagement for the ongoing protection of confidential information (e.g., assessment reports, progress reports). Chapter 6 covers these issues in more detail.

A CONTINUUM OF COMPLEXITY
OF COACHING SERVICES

As illustrated in the coaching complexity continuum (see Table 1.1), there are a variety of types of coaching engagements, primarily differentiated by the nature and level of complexity of the need and/or context. (Note that because the definition of coaching psychology used in this book focuses on individual leaders, coaching groups or teams are not included in this continuum or this book; many resources are available to explore team coaching: Hackman, 2002; Hawkins, 2012; McCauley et al., 2021; see also the Team Coaching Zone website at https://teamcoachingzone.com.) While there have been other ways of mapping out types of leadership coaching in organizational contexts (Frisch et al., 2012), in this book, we will be using a four-level continuum of coaching complexity. Level 1 includes short, focused types of engagements, such as helping a client improve a particular skill (e.g., delivering presentations or listening), or what we call *targeted behavioral coaching* (e.g., helping a client interpret 360-degree feedback or other assessment results and possibly extending those interpretations into drafting a development plan). A Level 1 engagement may involve meeting with the client's manager to align the development plan with expectations. Note that even relatively simple and short coaching engagements require significant training, preparation, and skill to deliver effectively.

An example of a Level 1 coaching engagement as part of a larger leadership development program is the following:

> Anne was a properly trained and experienced internal coach at a financial services firm with a long tradition of using internal coaches as part of their middle management leadership development programs. Those programs used a 360-degree feedback questionnaire to provide feedback to participants and as a foundation for drafting an individual development plan (IDP). Interpretation of feedback results and drafting the IDP occurred during three coaching meetings, and the internal coaching team took on the required number of participants so that each participant had a coach.

Table 1.1

Coaching Complexity Continuum: Coaching Interventions Arranged by Complexity and the Likelihood of Internal or External Delivery of Coaching

Level 1	Level 2	Level 3	Level 4
Targeted behavioral coaching	Transition coaching	Executive coaching	Trusted leader advisor
■ One-on-one targeted skill development (e.g., presentations, listening, giving feedback)	■ Short program (3–6 months), limited number of sessions aimed at helping a newly hired/promoted executive make an efficient and productive transition to the new role	Full coaching engagement, 6 to 12 months or more, focused on	Open-ended time frame, customized advisory consultation
■ Interpretation of feedback—360 and from leadership training		■ Enhancing current managerial or leadership performance or remediating an issue or obstacle	■ CP serves as thought partner, "sounding board," facilitating client's thinking, working through client's unique and complex leadership challenges
■ Client's responses to self-insight questionnaire or simulation exercises		■ Readiness for future opportunities, often linked with the organization's talent management/leader succession plan	■ Client is typically a C-level executive
May include:	May draw upon insight, feedback, and transition planning tools		■ Emphasis is less likely to be on stakeholders, development tools, and formal development planning
■ Planning for individual development action plan	■ Transition/assimilation: more complex—e.g., first international assignment, repatriation, other major change (e.g., higher level executive role)		
■ Scheduled follow-up meetings/calls focused on progress in implementing development action plan			

Note. CP = coaching psychologist. From *Becoming an Exceptional Executive Coach: Use Your Knowledge, Experience, and Intuition to Help Leaders Excel* (p. 35), by M. H. Frisch, R. J. Lee, K. L. Metzger, J. Robinson, and J. Rosemarin, 2012, AMACOM. Copyright 2012 by Michael H. Frisch. Adapted with permission.

Participants in these programs often rated their coaching experience as the high point of the training experience.

Level 2 coaching, *transition coaching*, is aimed at client skill strengthening for moving into a new organization or transitioning into a significantly new and/or higher level role in their current organization. This level of engagement is usually structured around a 3-month timeline, and it often yields a transition plan that management and HR sponsors are expected to follow up on from time to time as the client implements it. As an example, consider the case of Marvin, a professional engineer:

> Marvin had been with a large manufacturing company for 10 years and had advanced quickly to be the top engineer, well respected for his deep and broad knowledge of engineering, patented designs, analytical and problem-solving abilities, and strong work ethic. He was the go-to person for all things related to engineering design and manufacturing processes. Marvin had three children who would soon be preparing for college, and he had aspirations for advancement into management, primarily for greater salary and benefits. On his own initiative, he had taken several company training courses in management and leadership. Management recognized his value to the company and promoted him to the plant manager position in one of their manufacturing facilities.
>
> It was a difficult transition. Productivity at that plant was considered by management to be well below expectations and engineering and production to be mediocre to substandard. One of the most irritating things to Marvin was that people popped into his office all day long, asking how he wanted something done, requesting resources, reporting behavior problems with coworkers, and so on. He was increasingly irritated that he "couldn't get his work done" because people were interrupting him all day long, and frequently he had to go onto the shop floor to solve problems and show people how to do things. It was especially difficult to have engineering done by people who were far less educated and skilled than he, and his "teaching them" only worked for the particular thing he was teaching them how to do. Marvin's manager, who had worked with a CP for several years, saw his frustration and recommended that he get

individual executive coaching to help him make the transition into leadership and management a little easier.

Marvin and his coach took a step back from his tactical challenges and examined Marvin's transition in six key areas: the responsibilities and accountabilities of the plant manager job, his leadership strengths and gaps, his relationship with his manager, his current team, his peers in the wider organization, and his resources outside his organization in his industry. Together they mapped out transition challenges and opportunities under these six topics and shaped a transition plan that Marvin got his manager's support in implementing. Continuing to apply what he had learned in coaching, Marvin ended up changing many aspects of his work style, including how he saw "his work" (that of manager), moving "out of the weeds" and into managing, including doing a better job of expectation setting with his team and actively working to develop their skills.

Level 3 coaching, full *executive coaching*, includes the most familiar forms, typically spanning between 6 and 12 months, sometimes longer (Vandaveer et al., 2016). These engagements focus on identifying significant leadership strengths and planning how best to leverage them further and identifying key focus areas for development to enhance the leader's effectiveness. In addition to elevating effectiveness in the leader's current role, Level 3 coaching may also include preparation of the leader for a possible future role, helping them work toward realizing their potential to advance to higher levels of organizational leadership. A focus on the issues and leadership challenges in the current role goes back to the early days of coaching when fix-it or remedial coaching predominated. By contrast, leadership coaching today has strongly shifted toward more positive, upside coaching for leaders identified as having high potential. The relative emphasis on current or future job is important to discuss during contracting and in the early stages of coaching to focus development work appropriately. An example of Level 3 coaching is the case of Joan:

Joan was a vice-president in a large global consumer products company. She had risen through the ranks from marketing professional to product management, advancing quickly from overseeing small, then medium-size products lines to managing the company's largest, most recognized product and brand. She had recently received a big promotion to vice-president, reporting to the CEO. Along the way, she had spent 6 months in the finance and administration department and 12 months in a special assignment as chief of staff for the CEO. In that role, she obtained the "big picture" view of the entire company; all communications, requests, and deliverables to the CEO went through her for review, triage, and briefing the CEO. Following that assignment, she was promoted to the vice-president position. Joan aspired to be the next CEO after the current CEO's retirement. She had 5 years to prepare, and the CEO had suggested that she engage an executive CP. On the recommendation from a colleague and friend in a different company, Joan engaged Susan for executive coaching.

Joan felt positive and optimistic about her chances of succeeding her manager, and she enthusiastically made room in her schedule for 2-hour coaching meetings every other week. She and Susan connected well immediately. As part of the process of coaching, Susan interviewed 12 of Joan's "key stakeholders" (i.e., supervisor, peer colleagues, direct reports) to gather feedback for Joan helpful for informing their work together. The short story is that Joan was surprised by the feedback from her key stakeholders, with the exception of her manager, who thought she "walked on water." Others saw her as cold, narcissistic, brutally competitive, and feared by those who reported to her. The interviewees who had known her for many years reported that she had changed significantly over the years— from someone who was friendly, caring, sensitive to others' feelings, and empathetic to (now) someone they hardly recognized as the same person. Not only was Joan shocked by the feedback, but she was also shaken that she had such a big "blind spot" that she hadn't noticed others' reactions to her had changed. The CP was engaged for 6 months, at the end of which Joan and her manager extended the term to an additional 6 months of coaching. Susan used a cognitive-behavioral and a gestalt approach in coaching (described in Chapter 3) to uncover some blind spots, stimulate fresh insights, and help Joan make some significant changes in the mindset that was helping to drive her behavior.

As you can see, this Level 3 coaching example was a more complex situation that required greater experience and expertise on the part of the CP and a longer time to achieve Joan's goals.

Note that as the CP develops their expertise through experience and ongoing professional development learning, over time, the "art part" of coaching blossoms, and the approach and specific steps taken evolve to match the client's learning style, particular constellation of leadership strengths, and personal characteristics of the client—and the personal style and talents of the CP. Coaching often becomes more process oriented (always goal focused) and more a journey of discovery, learning, and breakthrough accomplishment than specified structured steps. Often, the client who learns and responds better to this approach achieves far more than initially targeted. As the CP "hits their stride" in effectiveness in coaching leaders, coaching engagements can evolve into a Level 4 relationship with the client in which the CP becomes a trusted leadership advisor (Wasylyshyn, 2015).

Level 4 advisory consultation, serving as *a trusted leadership advisor* (Wasylyshyn, 2015), is the most open-ended and least-structured type of individualized executive and leader consultation, conducted by a highly experienced CP—often following a Level 3 executive coaching engagement. Senior leaders often find that having a trusted CP to confer with as an impartial sounding board and thought partner can be invaluable. Being at the top of an organization (C-suite, as in chief executive officer or chief operating officer) can be isolating and the pressures great. This type of role has gained traction with CPs in recent years (Kaney, 2017; Wasylyshyn, 2014, 2015, 2017, 2019; White, 2006). Level 1 and Level 2 coaching have fewer moving parts, and the engagements are typically short in duration, whereas Level 3 coaching typically involves more stakeholders and process steps and may also involve work at deeper levels of conscious and subconscious awareness. Level 4 advisory consultation engagements are all different by their nature and typically involve a wider and deeper range of focus areas. They are engagements of longer duration and nearly always have an even greater impact on the organization (Wasylyshyn, 2014).

The continuum of complexity of coaching has implications for whether the engagement is likely to be delivered by an internal or external coach—and whether by a nonpsychologist coach or CP. *Internal coaching*—that is, coaching delivered by a professional who is an employee of the client organization, usually someone in leadership development or other TM areas of HR (Frisch, 2001)—is becoming increasingly common in larger organizations. There is evidence that internal coaches have contextual knowledge that can help them be even more effective than external coaches (Jones et al., 2016). However, the importance of understanding the level of coaching required and contracted for applies equally whether the engagement is delivered by internal or external coaches. One consistent difference in contracting between internal and external coaches is how the coach is paid for services. We have observed that internal coaches are much more likely to deliver coaching Levels 1 and 2, and external coaches are more likely to deliver coaching Level 3. This is consistent with the degree of complexity, professional time and level of coaching expertise and experience required, confidentiality, and other factors. This is simply an observation of typical practice; it should not be considered a limitation.

The descriptions of these four levels of coaching engagements are not meant to be rigidly confining—quite the opposite. We have observed and encourage creativity in applying coaching to help in unusual contexts and unique client situations. As CPs internalize what is unique about each coaching engagement, they are better able to expand their repertoire to help clients and organizations deal with the changing nature of work. Building on that point, we believe that spreading out levels of coaching along a continuum of complexity also provides easier understanding for newer practitioners about how to build experience and skills. Aspiring executive coaches sometimes feel intimidated as they observe highly experienced colleagues delivering coaching Level 3 and evolving to advisory consultation Level 4 as a trusted leadership advisor. This taxonomy of coaching complexity is a helpful guide for how to go from no or little coaching experience to those high-profile engagements. The coaching complexity continuum is intended to serve as a road map for growing as a professional CP, and it should help match coaching engagements with the level of coach training and experience. The nomenclature is intended to serve as a foundation on which to build rather than as a boundary that blocks experience.

SUMMARY

In this chapter, coaching psychology was described and compared with the other psychology-based helping services of therapy and counseling as well as leader mentoring. The comparison factors were each area's purpose, focus, context and nature of the work, and supporting theoretical foundations. A continuum of complexity of individual coaching engagements was presented, describing the nature of coaching at each level and the general level of coaching psychology expertise required for effectiveness at each level.

In Chapter 2, we look more closely at what a CP actually does. We describe the steps in a typical coaching engagement (Level 3 coaching) from beginning to end. Then, in Chapter 3, we look more closely at the methods, coaching models, and learning aids used to help the coaching client learn and develop to achieve their coaching goals.

2

A Closer Look: The Coaching Psychology Engagement

Now that we have considered the role of coaching as a key component of leader development, let's turn to what the coaching psychologist actually does—from beginning to end—in the coaching engagement.

THE COACHING ENGAGEMENT: A BIG-PICTURE OVERVIEW

The following seven phases make up the coaching process:

1. initial inquiry about or request for coaching services,
2. next-step meeting(s),
3. contracting the coaching engagement,
4. managing the coaching engagement,
5. coaching,

https://doi.org/10.1037/0000293-003
Coaching Psychology: Catalyzing Excellence in Organizational Leadership, by V. V. Vandaveer and M. H. Frisch

6. concluding the engagement, and
7. follow-up and evaluation.

Figure 2.1 portrays the process along a timeline, from the beginning (initial requests) to the conclusion, follow-up and evaluation (Frisch, 2019). A critically important part of a successful coaching engagement, of course, is managing the process, conceptualized as an arc in the center of Figure 2.1. However, events at various levels of organizational intervention are happening both before and after the arc of the actual coaching engagement.

INITIAL INQUIRY ABOUT OR REQUEST FOR COACHING SERVICES

Before the engagement begins, there are many ways a coaching psychologist (CP) might be contacted by an organization for leader development coaching, including through human resources (HR) or talent management (TM), through a leader who seeks coaching for themselves or a direct report, as part of a leadership development program, or associated with a larger organizational consulting engagement (e.g., change management, team development, organization development).

If the CP is internal to the organization and is qualified and if Level 1 or Level 2 coaching is needed, they may provide that service. If the CP is with a consulting firm that provides coaching services, coaching clients are likely to come to them from the firm's managing partners. However, if the firm does not currently provide coaching services but is open to offering them, the partners may introduce the qualified CP to the appropriate people in their client's organization, which is a great opportunity for the firm to break into the coaching space.

If the CP is an independent consultant who is doing organizational consulting, opportunities for individual coaching often arise out of the consulting work. Sometimes organizations send out a request for a proposal for coaching services to which a CP can respond. In our experience, however, most individual coaching is not initiated that way. More likely is finding a CP through word of mouth, a referral from an existing client,

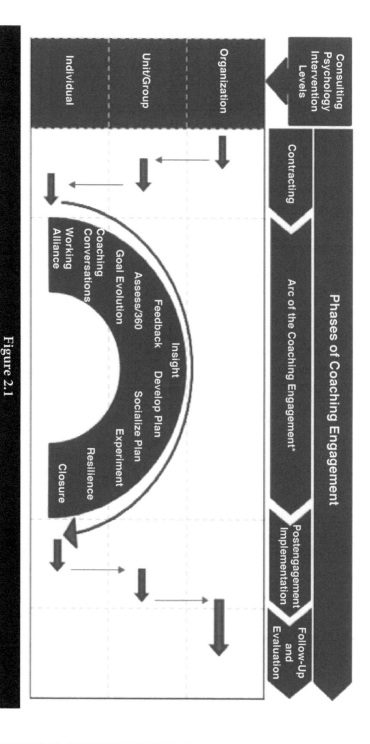

Figure 2.1

The arc of the coaching engagement. *The arc of the coaching engagement may extend upward to the Organization intervention level if the coaching client has an organizationwide leadership role. From *Coaching Psychology: Consulting Psychology Interventions at the Level of the Individual* [Unpublished monograph], by M. H. Frisch, 2019. Copyright 2019 by M. H. Frisch. Used with permission.

or consulting work with the client organization that needs coaching. In any case, a representative from the client organization (e.g., from HR, TM, or an individual manager who wishes to explore leadership development coaching) will at some point contact the CP directly about the coaching need.

A clinical or counseling psychologist in private practice may get a request for coaching from a therapy patient or client or from someone a therapy patient referred to the CP for coaching. (Chapters 5 and 6 address this type of request in more detail.)

In early conversations with organizational representatives, the CP learns what the client's general need is and presents their coaching experience, approach, and availability. If the contact client (Schein, 1999; see also Chapter 1, this volume) sees a potential match between the CP's capabilities and the development need, the CP may be referred to the sponsor(s) (primary clients) of the coaching engagement: the potential coaching client's manager and perhaps also someone in TM or HR. The potential client's manager is, of course, responsible for developing direct reports, and the manager typically pays the bill and has approval authority for the coaching services (including coaching goals, development plans, duration of the coaching engagement, etc.). In larger companies with more sophisticated TM or HR functions, a TM or HR business partner may also have responsibility for monitoring individuals' development progress as part of their responsibility for managing leadership development (LD) programs.

In this book, we use the term *coaching client* or simply "the client" to refer to the person in the developmental relationship with the coach. The CP should be aware that by the time an organizational sponsor of coaching services has made contact, a lot has already happened. Key decisions have been made, such as determining whether coaching is the best approach to development at this time, what the organization is willing to invest in coaching services, criteria for selecting a coach (e.g., nature and depth of coach training, industry or sector specialization, alignment with the organization's coaching process expectations, diversity mix among coaches, practice specializations, and whether internal or external to the organization), and what the process will be for selecting a coach to work with a client. Sometimes, an enterprise coaching manager is designated to develop coaching standards, monitor applications and the vetting and hiring process, and monitor and evaluate coaching engagements across the organization. The organization's preparation for coaching also ideally includes communicating with all appropriate parts of the organization (e.g., levels of management, HR, LD) about coaching and its purposes and uses, how and on what bases individuals will be selected for coaching, and other considerations to help ensure that coaching will be a wise organizational investment and a positive experience for its leaders.

NEXT-STEP MEETINGS

Early meetings before the arc of the engagement begins often include the coach, the coaching client, and the client's manager for the purposes of (a) becoming acquainted and beginning the most important aspect of coaching—establishing effective relationships with both manager and coaching client; (b) engaging in dialogue about what the coaching client wants to accomplish in coaching, the manager's expressed desired outcomes, and possibly what leader developmental work the client has already done; (c) discussing the CP's general approach to coaching, especially in terms of process steps, typical nature of meetings with respect to content and frequency, and the "rules of engagement" (e.g., respective roles of all parties, deliverables, the extent of confidentiality); and (d) discussing the coaching client's preferred methods of learning. By far, the most important of these is the first one—establishing a strong and credible connection with the coaching client. As we elaborate in Chapter 3, the most important factor that is under the coach's control in achieving the desired outcomes in coaching is the quality of the relationship and the degree of connectedness established between client and CP. The CP candidate with whom the potential coaching client feels the strongest connection in the initial meeting will most likely be selected for the assignment. This also sets the stage for the working alliance that needs to take root as the arc of the coaching engagement begins (Graßmann et al., 2020; McKenna & Davis, 2009).

While we are on this topic, here is a tip for increasing the likelihood of being selected for the assignment: People feel the strongest connection with the person they feel best hears them. Spend more time polishing your listening-to-hear skill and connecting with the individual's "heart" than on preparing a slick "sales" speech about yourself.

CONTRACTING THE COACHING ENGAGEMENT

When a CP is selected to provide coaching services, the next step is the critically important process of contracting the engagement to be sure everyone is on the same page about the engagement.

Contracting in coaching psychology refers to the discussions that take place before coaching starts that define and frame the coaching engagement, including the roles of the various participants and rules of engagement (Lee, 2013).[1] More specifically, the CP, the coaching client, and the client's manager will articulate and agree on expectations for the process: steps, roles, time span, general outcomes, and deliverables, including what information will be kept strictly confidential between the CP and the coaching client; what will be shared with the manager and, if applicable, other sponsor(s); fees; and other relevant matters. In this step, the CP will also be seeking to learn even more about the needs of the coaching client: more detail about what the client needs or wants to accomplish, learn, or change and what "success" will look like—how it will be measured.

With respect to confidentiality, coaching conversations between client and coach are typically held in confidence, and the content is not shared by the coach, except as agreed in the beginning. This is done to ensure a safe psychological environment for the client and coach in which

---

[1]The term *contracting* is sometimes used in reference to setting coaching goals—for instance, "The client and I contracted to work on her time management skills." Although this is an appropriate term to use in this way, for clarity in this book, we only use the term *contracting* to refer to defining and agreeing to coaching process steps and rules of engagement in the beginning—and sometimes later in the process when adjustments to the initial agreement about process need to be made.

thoughts, possibilities, concerns, fears, problems and difficulties, and career aspirations can be discussed openly and on a personal level and effectively examined and addressed. Thus, executive coaching provides a secure environment for candid conversations about a wide range of topics, personal strategy formation, and problem solving about personal effectiveness as a leader.

There are some exceptions to the confidentiality rule, and the CP needs to be clear about what those are and how to handle them. Chapter 6 contains more about the confidentiality rule and exceptions.

Even the least complex, short-duration coaching engagements (Level 1) need to be carefully contracted, assuring agreement among sponsors, coaching clients, and CPs to ensure consistent understanding of the process, deliverables, timelines, and so on. Moving among variations of Level 1 coaching (assessment debrief coaching with or without follow-up appointments, possibly yielding a draft development plan) illustrates the importance of contracting even simple coaching engagements. Issues such as the number of follow-up appointments, the time frame to finish, how the development plan will be structured, what is confidential between coaching client and CP, and what will be shared with sponsors all need to be specified and agreed on. Organizations that are experienced sponsors of coaching often have worked out general process expectations and contractual elements, and they may have written them up as "statements of work" (SOWs) or "letters of agreement" (LOAs).

While all this may seem obvious, these items are "baseline." Many things can come up later in a coaching engagement that were not planned for in contracting and that can cause difficulties. A few examples include many more client-required meetings than assumed in the pricing; goal-related underlying issues surfaced in coaching that will take more work and more time than budgeted; manager turnover, and the new manager not apprised of the confidentiality agreement shares the assessment report with her management peers; and so forth. With experience, a CP learns what to anticipate and what to be sure to cover in contracting. Effective initial contracting facilitates deeper engagement and faster progress, and it helps prevent later problems that can derail or doom a coaching engagement. Effective contracting is well worth the time and effort required.

Although coaching can appear standardized in some organizations, each case is and should be treated as a unique engagement, with time invested by both coach and sponsors (often within the organization's TM function) to identify any unique elements or special requirements for each engagement.

During the contracting process (i.e., agreeing on the specifics and "rules" of the coaching engagement, which is different, by the way, from filling out a legal document), the CP may encounter missing or problematic information. Examples include an absent managerial sponsor, a pending reorganization, important needed feedback that has been withheld from the client, an extremely defensive client, or suspected misuse of coaching by the sponsor or manager of the prospective coaching client. Although most coaches press ahead and hope for the best, we highly recommend that in such cases, the CP slow down the contracting process and explore such concerns with primary clients and other sponsors. Two instances of such concerns that are showstoppers are (a) a client whose focus is consumed elsewhere by significant work, personal issues, or other pressures, rendering that person unable to give sufficient attention to professional development and (b) sponsors who indicate uncertainty about retaining the client at all. Occasionally (though not often in our experience), a primary client intends to fire the individual but wants to be able to show in the record that everything possible was done to save them, "even coaching." The CP must be on the lookout for such disingenuous solicitations of coaching services to develop an individual and, when detected, politely but firmly walk away. If the CP detects that the process they are about to sign up for is disingenuous, it will be important not to become involved in anything that could cause harm to the individual or the CP's reputation. See Chapter 6 for more examples of these challenges.

While the people for whom the company invests in individual executive coaching are typically already high performers who wish to become even more effective—or desire to advance to higher levels of leadership in the organization—in some cases, individuals who are making valuable contributions to the organization but have one or more problematic behaviors may also receive coaching because the company wants to retain them, assuming the individual's undesired impacts can be ameliorated or sufficiently minimized with coaching.

There are other potential derailers to a coaching assignment (Frisch, 2005a, 2005b; see also the example professional issues in Chapter 6). Sometimes, adjustments can be made to the process and associated contracting agreement that will ameliorate concerns, and coaching can proceed. If not, then it is best to delay or even decline the engagement. Once initial contracting is completed, the coaching work can begin.

MANAGING THE COACHING ENGAGEMENT

To explain the flow of what happens in a coaching engagement, we will use Level 3, executive coaching, as described in Table 1.1 in Chapter 1. These are typically 6- to 12-month leadership coaching engagements (Vandaveer et al., 2016). Figure 2.1 shows typical steps and milestones.

As Figure 2.1 shows, the arc of the coaching engagement progresses in time (horizontal axis of the arc), implying that the complexity of coaching increases (vertical axis), illustrated by the ascending arc. Inputs to the coaching process are added from stakeholders, both internal and external to the organization (e.g., feedback from manager, peers, direct reports, internal clients, external suppliers, consulting clients), and from other sources (e.g., leadership assessments, performance reviews, and/or observation of the client in management team meetings). The rich information gathered from these sources will inform and help focus the coaching work and evolving goals. How the client is perceived by others and the client's descriptions of the context (e.g., culture, manager, peers, demands of the role, perceived power dynamics) are typically pivotal sources of insights about the client's effectiveness and needs. From that information, the CP and client will identify key focus areas (KFAs) for coaching. Usually, these KFAs are incorporated into an overall leader development plan, reviewed and approved (sometimes called "socialized") with the manager (and potentially other stakeholders) so that everyone is on the same development page.

At that point, the arc of the coaching engagement begins to descend back toward the one-on-one work with the client to begin to implement the development plan. The CP and client in partnership begin preparing for the conclusion of the active coaching engagement and the client's continuing commitment to implement developmental actions that increase expertise and effectiveness as a leader after the conclusion of coaching.

COACHING THE CLIENT

With the arc of a typical coaching engagement summarized, let's look at what generally happens before and within the actual process of coaching to facilitate the client's learning and development. (Chapter 3 describes a deeper dive on the primary methods, models, and learning aids that the CP typically uses for effective coaching.)

Preparation

Getting ready for the initial coaching meetings begins with the preparation of the CP, which includes reviewing all the information provided—information about the coaching client and the organizational context in which the client seeks to be more effective, desired outcomes, felt needs, agreed rules of engagement, and so on—as well as any other information about the organization available publicly. Equally or even more important, preparation includes the CP conducting a self-assessment and ensuring their personal and professional readiness for the initial meeting.

The self-check should include the following: Do I have an open and organized mind, positive energy, and a clear focus on this client and this work? There must also be a general plan for the meeting: In addition to the client organization's desired outcomes and felt needs, what additional objectives might I, as the CP, have for this first meeting? What specific outcomes are needed for this coaching engagement to get the best possible start, and how will success be determined?

First Few Coaching Meetings

In the first few meetings, some CPs find it helpful to keep in mind three Cs that support the working alliance with the client: connection, context, and contracting (updating).

Connection

Effective coaching depends primarily on, among other things, building and maintaining a strong connection and trusting relationship with the client. Research on coaching outcomes has consistently shown that the quality of the client–coach relationship (connection) is the primary success factor that is under the coach's control (Behrendt et al., 2021; McKenna & Davis, 2009; Page & de Haan, 2014). Connecting deeply with the client is important for establishing a foundation of trust, which allows quickly getting "in sync" and facilitates full sharing and identification of the client's professional and personal aspirations and hopes (which research has shown leads to better outcomes; Boyatzis & Jack, 2018); concerns about the current role and/or certain work relationships and how they are perceived by key stakeholders (manager, peers, direct reports, and others); and fears or insecurities, as well as other things that may impact effectiveness and professional and personal aspirations. Connecting deeply also allows the CP to tune in to and recognize quickly what sparks the client's positive energy and passion and when they may be tending to drift or tune out. The CP needs to "go with the flow" of the client and be skilled in building on the positive energy, redirecting and/or challenging (in a caring, fully supportive-of-the-client way) when necessary and encouraging new and different ways of thinking. See de Haan's (2008) book *Relational Coaching: Journeys Toward Mastering One-to-One Learning*.

An effective coaching relationship—or *working alliance*—with the client is described in the common factors research on effective helping relationships. McKenna and Davis (2009) notably extended these findings to coaching, helping to connect coaching practice with long traditions of outcomes research in related fields. Client insight is sparked through facilitated self-reflection, which leads to learning and growth (Stout-Rostron, 2014). Recent neuroscience research using functional magnetic resonance imaging has emphasized and reinforced conventional wisdom that the positive connection built in these early coaching meetings is key to fostering client openness, curiosity, and trust, thereby avoiding the triggering of defensiveness by driving toward "constructive" feedback too quickly (Boyatzis & Jack, 2018). However, more recent research has shown that attributes of the coachee, such as hope, expectancy, self-efficacy, resilience, and mental well-being, mediate the relationship between the felt quality of the coaching relationship and outcomes. (See more in Chapter 4 on coaching evaluation research and mediators that are active.) New research on the so-called common factors has suggested that they are not uniformly effective over the whole arc of a typical leadership-coaching engagement; application of the common factors appears to be much more important early in the engagement than later (de Haan et al., 2020).

Context

As mentioned in Chapter 1, a key distinction between coaching and clinical therapy is that the former is focused on helping clients become more effective in their (organizational) contexts. If a client were in another organization, the requirements for being effective and their responses to the culture, among other things, would be somewhat different (and sometimes a lot different).

Organizational contexts are social systems (De Cremer et al., 2012; Katz & Kahn, 1978) in which the client must be effective. Therefore, the CP must understand the dynamics of being a leader in a specific business, social, and organizational context; early meetings with the client must include beginning to learn as much as possible about the context from the client's and their sponsors' perspectives. In addition, if feedback from key stakeholders is collected later, an even richer, more in-depth understanding of the client's context will be acquired. This is where a coach's experience, training, and education in organizational structures, social systems and power dynamics, and leadership and in-depth familiarity with the leader's "job" inform the understanding of what is required to be effective in that role and organization. An example of the client's organizational context pertains to the power dynamics, which are social psychological in nature (De Cremer et al., 2012; Pfeffer, 2010); the leader or executive client will need to be effective in navigating those dynamics. Understanding the context is necessary for effectively finalizing the contracting between coach and organizational sponsors.

Contracting

Although the third C, contracting, has been established before the engagement begins, there are often elements of the coaching process that were not fully contracted in the beginning, such as whom to include in key stakeholder feedback, when to collect that feedback and by what means, and whether to do leadership psychological assessments. Thus, contracting continues during the engagement. That is, adjustments and additions may be suggested and added at any time during coaching. After coach and client discuss and agree about process adjustments, sponsor input and agreement must be sought in the spirit of process openness.

Goal Evolution

The felt needs and preliminary goals described at the beginning of the engagement will evolve as coaching progresses and the CP and client connect the leadership goals with the client's aspirations and learn more about the client's potential, stand-out talents and capabilities, and unique pattern of attributes; perceptions by key others; what needs to happen to achieve their potential and desired career path; and so on. The preliminary goals likely arose from the individual's sense of what they need to develop or strengthen and/or from other sources, such as performance reviews, TM processes, supervisors' assessments, 360-degree feedback, or other external sources. For example, a sponsor may say, "She needs to change this, do less of X, and do more of Y." Preliminary goals are often expressed in overly broad terms (e.g., "become a better leader" or "improve executive presence") and typically lack grounding in the client's context. The most effective CPs use those as starting points for the discovery of (a) superordinate or more well-defined goals that tap the client's aspirations and dreams and therefore are highly motivating (Boyatzis & Jack, 2018; Boyatzis & McKee, 2005; Dixit & Dixit, 2018), (b) root causes of the felt needs that are the appropriate target (or targets) for coaching work, and (c) sufficient clarity around (a) and (b) that "what success will look like" can be specified, as well as the key factors for achieving those goals. It is also the case that what has been identified as a weakness that needs strengthening may not be the right target for coaching. Working with the client will often be akin to peeling an onion, revealing more insights into the client's strengths and limitations, including what drives them (i.e., values, attitudes, and beliefs that drive behaviors and shape mindsets). Thus, felt needs and preliminary goals morph into positive, clearly stated client-owned expressions of development goals—one of the early milestones achieved that paves the way for rich learning and positive action.

As research in neuroscience has discovered, goals positively expressed that resonate with the client's aspirations and are grounded in the client's context will have a positive motivational effect on the client, infusing the CP–client work with positive energy for inspired client–partner discovery and insights that catalyze learning and growth (Boyatzis & Jack, 2018). For example, if a felt need is for the client to "stop micromanaging," that original goal might evolve into "build skill in empowering my staff, helping them grow and develop through effective delegation of responsibilities, which will help me accomplish much more and help position me much better for advancement to higher levels of management." Or it might become "learn to set the goals and direction (the 'what'), and let my team figure out the 'how,' and I will be open to different ways of doing things, which will result in increased morale in my team and higher productivity of my group, as well as a higher rating of my potential, making promotion more likely."

Note that as insight occurs and goals evolve, contracting may need to be updated. For example, say the CP and client are past the middle of the arc (Figure 2.1) and are processing feedback from key stakeholders and are preparing to finalize key focus areas for coaching, and they discover that a root cause of a behavior that needs to be strengthened or changed is something that will likely require more time and intense focus than what remains in the contract. Although this is probably not a frequent occurrence, it does happen, and when it does, it will need to be discussed with the client's manager and sponsors, and adjustments will have to be made accordingly if, for example, more time (and/or budget) will be required or work on other things postponed for a bit. Most of the time, informing the manager and other sponsors of the clearer, more specific goals that have evolved is not necessary because the CP and client are still working on the (more macro) goals they've approved, and it could be the case that the specifics of what they are working on to get there do not need to be shared.

Here's an example:

> Jane was a mid-level manager in XYZ consumer products company. She was exceptionally bright and highly business oriented and had the reputation of getting things done. However, she also had the reputation of having left a lot of broken glass in her wake. She clearly favored people who were like herself, and being bright was the main criterion of worthiness in her eyes. Her 360-degree feedback was pretty damning with respect to interpersonal relationships. She was provided the opportunity to work with a CP, which she eagerly embraced because she was extremely ambitious and looking to get to the vice-president level by the next year. Among other things, the CP administered a battery of leadership and organizational effectiveness assessments to possibly help explain others' perceptions. One of the assessments was a test of emotional intelligence (EI) as an ability. She scored below average on EI (general population norms), and aspects of her personality, as measured by other assessment instruments, were consistent with that finding (e.g., below-average empathy, strong dominance, tough minded, as opposed to sensitive and a high need for power). The felt-need goals included (from her manager) "needs to stop steamrolling over people and leaving broken glass." The evolved goal was to "improve awareness of and management of impact on others." That included work at the level of drivers and causes (see next section) and removing blind spots (i.e., things others saw about her behaviors that she didn't see). Note that individual assessment results (e.g., the personality assessment results) are private and confidential between CP and client, as specified in the contracting phase, and they were not shared with her manager. She and her coach were working on the evolved ("negotiated") goal, and what they specifically worked on in private together to achieve that goal was confidential so that they could work with complete candor, with the coach being fully supportive and, at the same time, able to challenge. A strong connection and trust had been established between coach and client, and Jane made good progress toward her evolved goal, which resulted

in observable improvement in the original goal of "not steamrolling over people," which was important to the manager.

Although the work in Level 1 and Level 2 coaching is behavioral in nature, Level 3 coaching work will typically be at deeper psychological levels of motivational drivers and causes. These then typically become focal points for coaching work, informing the work to best leverage key strengths and bring subconscious drivers, motives, or causes into consciousness to yield insights into how best to improve weaker aspects of performance. These dynamics are discussed more fully in Chapter 3 as part of the elaboration on the typical methods CPs use in coaching.

Providing Feedback

Providing feedback to the client is an important aspect of coaching at all levels (Behrendt et al., 2021; Gregory & Levy, 2015). Feedback includes (a) helping the client understand qualitative 360-degree feedback or standardized assessment results, (b) the CP sharing observations about the client's patterns of thinking and behavior, and (c) the CP's and others' observations of positive change. Clients often report that the comprehensive feedback gathered and interpreted with the coach is a high point of the coaching engagement. Having established a strong connection and a trusting relationship with the CP and knowing that the CP is fully in their corner, the client typically receives well otherwise difficult-to-get feedback that, as part of coaching, is provided in a safe and supportive environment. Feedback is used exclusively for the client's development; there are no administrative connections to HR files or performance appraisals. A coach's summary of informational interviews and any other assessment reports exist within the confidential domain of the coaching engagement, shared only between coach and client. However, an executive summary of the client's 360-degree feedback, prepared by the CP and with the client's agreement, may be provided to the client's manager if agreed to in the contracting phase. This structure supports the coach being complete and direct in summarizing the key messages of feedback and the client's confidence that the information is honest and comprehensive.

Chapter 3 addresses feedback more completely as a key coaching tool.

Development Planning

Coach and client collaborate in drafting a development plan. Such plans are created knowing that they will be a primary tangible deliverable from the coaching engagement that will be shared with sponsors. Helping the client summarize strengths is important because creating such a summary is surprisingly difficult for some clients. As goals evolve with input from the feedback process, the CP can assist in phrasing them positively, consistent with the client's now clear sense of what to work on—that is, identifying the way forward in the development journey. To note progress, now further-evolved goals will be entered into the development plan as action objectives. Usually, there is a direct conceptual connection between the original felt needs and these action objectives, phrased as positive aspirations with clear implications for in-the-context actions. Tying them back to felt needs is an important final step so that sponsors will readily see that the goals are on target and, therefore, actively supported by the sponsors. In cases where the finalized goals differ considerably from the initial goals—most often due to the discovery of "root cause" issues that must be worked on—the sponsors will have been informed earlier in the process what the target goals are that better achieve the superordinate general goal of overall enhanced leader effectiveness. Focus areas for action will have been identified for each development goal. Together, CP and client produce a well-founded, balanced, and motivating development plan ready to be shared with sponsors. (For examples of formats for the development plan if the client organization doesn't have one that it uses, see Frisch et al., 2012.)

Finalizing the client's development plan is positively reinforcing for the client because it is a tangible sign of progress and makes the path to goal achievement clear (Frisch et al., 2012). A development planning meeting (DPM) with the client's manager and any other sponsor is aimed at socializing the development plan and gaining consensus on the way forward. In that meeting, the client will review the draft plan with them, ask for their perspectives, and discuss any elements they feel are missing so that a consensus can be achieved. The updated development plan is a concise summary of the goals that will guide the client's learning and development. How the client and CP arrived at the key focus areas and goals, what they discussed, and the data they explored, reframed, and captured remains in the confidential part of the coaching process. The product of that safety and rigor is a developmental action plan that is clear and detailed enough so that all parties can make whatever adjustments are needed for complete alignment and to foster sponsors' full support.

While the client takes the lead in their own DPM, the CP's presence in this meeting, or meetings, is useful in two ways. First, the CP can support the client as needed in talking through the plan, ensuring that the conversation highlights the client's strengths to be leveraged in service of developing other areas and asking questions such as "When do you see those strengths in action?" "What strengths are you aware of that are not shown in the plan?" There are other places in the meeting when a question from the CP can deepen the conversation—for example, "What other action ideas do you have to help facilitate progress toward goals?" Second, the CP's actively participating in the meeting allows CP and client to later debrief it for any learning from observations of and interactions with sponsors. There are often elements of the development plan that tie behaviorally to the DPM (e.g., asserting, listening, influencing), and the CP's presence allows those to be tapped for the client's insight and manager's observation. Finally, toward the end of a DPM, the next steps in coaching are often confirmed, along with the expected time until closure.

In the coaching meetings after the DPM, the CP and client actively debrief the client's goals, the resulting adjustments to the plan, and what the client will do postcoaching to ensure sustained commitment to the ongoing implementation of their development plan. They also begin contemplating the wrap-up of the coaching engagement. This emphasizes that the client's ongoing learning and development is a lifelong journey. The CP and client can speculate about unknowns and possible derailers of the client's developmental efforts and anticipate how to prevent them or rebound if they occur. Planning for ways to obtain ongoing feedback and ensuring that the client has a development discussion at least annually with the manager will be important.

In addition, a final meeting (sometimes called a *bookend meeting*) can be arranged near the end of the coaching engagement with those who participated in the DPM. The client, who is responsible for their ongoing development, should lead that conversation (with prior preparation with the CP), discussing sponsors' observed progress and any needed adjustments in the development plan. The client and sponsors should reaffirm their respective roles in commitment to the client's ongoing development. This meeting also serves as the formal successful conclusion of the coaching engagement. As the CP's direct involvement is ending, the sponsors, especially the client's manager, need to reinforce and support the client's commitment to keeping the momentum going. These guidelines apply equally to internal and external coaches, even though internal coaches may have later informal or casual contact with clients. In some ways, this makes closure even more important for internal coaches to signal the unambiguous close to the engagement, while the relationship may continue but in a different form.

To summarize, final coaching meetings can be fruitful opportunities to reflect, celebrate progress, and formalize plans and mechanisms for ongoing learning and development and sustaining the positive changes. If the client has requested occasional follow-up check-ins with the CP, and if the manager has approved, contracting for those can be done at this point.

It should be noted here that Level 3 coaching engagements have varying degrees of structure, and some are or become more of a continuing process of discovery and learning. The important thing to remember is that everything needs to be clearly contracted in the beginning, and as changes are contemplated, the contracting must be updated before making the changes.

CONCLUDING THE ENGAGEMENT

With an agreed plan in place and the CP and client having openly prepared for the conclusion of the formal coaching engagement, the client will continue implementing the plan, seeking feedback from time to time from the manager or others. It is never too early in coaching to be sure that closure is in the client's awareness of the process. Indeed, it is part of the earliest conversations for Level 1 and Level 2 coaching because those engagements are short. Clients benefit from awareness that the engagement has an arc to it, and many report that they experienced satisfaction and a sense of accomplishment in passing the milestones toward closure. Preparing and equipping the client for ongoing self-development is the primary objective of the final coaching meeting, and the meeting represents the commencement of new beginnings toward the desired future.

FOLLOW-UP AND EVALUATION OF THE COACHING ENGAGEMENT

Learning continues for everyone after a coaching engagement—the client, the client's manager, other sponsors, and the CP. We recommend that the CP and client jointly evaluate their work: What went especially well, what were the high points, and what could have gone better and how? Organizations have a keen interest in assessing the effectiveness of their development dollars, and many have an evaluation process in place, administered postengagement. If they do not, we recommend that CPs request feedback from managers and sponsors in a structured way. Some find it helpful to create a feedback template for the coaching client and their sponsors to use for providing feedback, anonymously or not, to the CP. There is certainly a growing published literature about coaching evaluation (see Chapter 4). These studies are not possible without organizational support to collect the necessary data. The immense value to the organization, the coach, and the discipline of coaching cannot be underestimated.

Following the conclusion of the coaching engagement, some coaches periodically check in with the client to see how things are going. It is especially important if this is done to include it in the contracting document from the beginning. This will likely not be billed work—unless a part of the SOW or the client requests an extension of coaching, in which case the original contracted SOW will be updated. The rationale for periodic, unbilled follow-up includes (a) reinforcement of the client's commitment to sustaining the positive changes and ongoing self-development—just by hearing from the CP occasionally—and (b) invaluable feedback for the CP about longer term effects and sustainability of coaching, allowing for the coach's own continued growth and improvement.

Note that if follow-up is not included in contracting, it can be problematic in several ways for the CP to reach back to clients after coaching has concluded. It can be perceived as a lack of confidence in the client or as an attempt to sell more coaching, and it might unsettle the client in other ways. Follow-up contact should be agreed to while the coaching is still active, with the mutual understanding that clients can reach out but that it is not part of the coach's role to do so in an unscheduled manner.

In some circumstances, clients actively request that coaching be extended for a time or to help with a specific challenging situation. In these cases, and when the manager and other sponsors agree, the CP will work with the client and sponsors to develop an addendum to the original SOW or develop a new one, again specifying the purpose, felt needs and desired outcomes, work products, and fees. CPs must not have a personal stake in a client's request for extension (e.g., to keep the income stream flowing), and in most cases, clients prefer to move on from coaching, feeling satisfied having achieved—and perhaps exceeded—the desired goals, which has well prepared them for ongoing, lifelong learning, knowing that they can always reengage in coaching if they so desire.

SUMMARY

This chapter featured (a) management of the coaching engagement, aided by the conceptualization of an arc along a timeline that guides the coaching process; (b) at a high level, the process of coaching (i.e., facilitating the client's learning and development); (c) illustrations of the different kinds of clients a CP has in a coaching engagement; and (d) the conclusion of the engagement, including the final meeting and ensuring that the client is prepared for and committed to the ongoing implementation of their development plan and (if previously contracted for) reiterating the plans for follow-up.

In Chapter 3, we take a deeper dive into the intricacies of coaching clients, describing the tools, methods, and techniques that the CP can draw on to facilitate client learning and development.

3

Coaching Psychology Tools, Methods, and Techniques

The best investment is in the tools of one's own trade.

—Benjamin Franklin

Having clarified in Chapter 1 the primary differentiators of coaching psychology versus therapy, counseling, and mentoring and the typical coaching process in Chapter 2, this chapter focuses on the tools, methods, and techniques that the coaching psychologist (CP) typically uses to facilitate the coaching client's learning effectively.

TOOLS

The CP's Self

The most important and primary tool for the CP is the CP's self. The CP is the primary "instrument" for facilitating the client's learning and

https://doi.org/10.1037/0000293-004
Coaching Psychology: Catalyzing Excellence in Organizational Leadership, by V. V. Vandaveer and M. H. Frisch

development and in that role selects, develops, administers, and interprets the outputs of all the other tools, ensuring their effectiveness and proper use for and by the client (Bachkirova, 2016; Courtney & Vandaveer, 2013; Frisch, 2008; Stevenson, 2004; Vandaveer, 2012b). Bachkirova (2016) provided insight into the CP's self as an instrument in supporting client development:

> The nature of coaching requires that the CP practitioners connect with clients on a personal level, creating a relationship in which trust is based not only on the coach's skills and knowledge but also on the [client's] feeling that the coach is fundamentally on the client's side and a trustworthy human being in this relationship. (p. 144)

Bachkirova (2016) distinguished between the *competent self* (i.e., CP expertise about the process of coaching, skills, tools, and other coach competencies) and the *dialogic self* (the CP as a partner in dialogue and collaborative engagement in joint meaning making, in which attention is given to implicit intentions behind words). The use of both competent and dialogic selves is essential in coaching. However, Bachkirova posited that the dialogic self, which is less structured and more open-ended, may be the most impactful for the client:

> I would argue that the interventions of the coach are initiated not only from the knowledge and understanding of the clients' situation, context, psychological makeup, and goals but also from the personal resonating with all of these in the moment and, therefore, from the self of the coach. (p. 144)

An example of a statement that the CP might make using the dialogic self is:

> In your 360 feedback, your direct reports and your manager described your relational skills as "stand-out strengths," but your peer colleagues rated your effectiveness as moderately or sometimes effective. Do you have any insight into what your peers are seeing that your manager is not? How should we interpret this?

(This is an example of the CP and client engaging in joint meaning making.) As coaching experience builds and the CP–client relationship becomes stronger, the CP and client can examine together more emotionally charged issues that surface.

Note that the use of self does not include the coach sharing stories from the coach's life or examples from other engagements. Although these may be relevant, they are not part of the use of self in coaching and should be used sparingly and purposefully, if at all. It is important always to remember that coaching is about the client, not the coach.

As with any tool, self in coaching requires continual sharpening. This includes keeping up-to-date on findings from research and practice as well as investing in expanding both the competent self and dialogic self. A highly effective way to enhance these skills is for every CP to engage periodically and regularly with a coach supervisor or peer consultant to debrief actual work with clients. This professional development activity is an essential part of continuous learning in all the helping professions, including executive coaching. Peer consultation for coaches is rapidly becoming a foundational aspect of coaching skill development. (See the comments on peer consultation in Chapter 6.)

The CP–Client Relationship

As mentioned in Chapter 2, a substantial body of research shows that the quality of the relationship between the CP and client is among the most important factors in the success of the coaching engagement (Cox et al., 2014; de Haan et al., 2013, 2020; De Meuse et al., 2009; McKenna & Davis, 2009; Rousmaniere et al., 2017; Tracey et al., 2014; Vandaveer, 2017). Therefore, the importance of continually building and refining expertise in the dialogic self cannot be overstated.

Behrendt et al. (2021) conceptualized three metatypes of coach behavior that combine to move coaching clients toward goal attainment: relationship-oriented behaviors, purpose-oriented behaviors, and change-warranting behaviors. *Relationship-oriented behaviors* align with the common factors research, *purpose-oriented behaviors* foster client motivation and focus, and *change-warranting behaviors* can be thought of as the use of self and providing feedback. CPs may find that this overall conceptualization helps bring together important ideas about the coach–client relationship, and in fact, the authors labeled it as an integrative model.

Research has also showed that attributes of the client outside of the coaching relationship (e.g., openness to experience and feedback, learning orientation, self-efficacy, self-awareness) are strong predictors of coaching effectiveness, accounting for 40% of the variance in outcomes, followed closely by the quality of the coach–client relationship (i.e., to the extent coaching is focused on goals and topics most important to the client and the quality of the affective bond established between the client and CP) as the next most important factor, accounting for 30% of the variance in outcomes. Client expectancy and hope, theory and techniques each accounted for 15% of the variance in outcomes (McKenna & Davis, 2009). These factors have been referred to as *common factors* in effective helping relationships (Baron & Morin, 2010; de Haan et al., 2013; McKenna & Davis, 2009). However, more recent research has raised a caveat that the usefulness of relying on common factors is greater earlier in the arc of the coaching engagement than later (de Haan et al., 2020).

Naturally, people who aspire to become CPs vary on many dimensions of self, and there is no one "best profile." With so many variables in clients, engagements, contexts, and coaches, a unique and complex interplay of factors determines the effectiveness of a particular CP–client partnership. Every CP will have strengths, limitations, and development needs. It is essential for the CP to have self-insight about their strengths, limitations, and impact, gained through feedback, introspection, continuous learning, and a professional helping relationship for themselves (e.g., coach, peer consultant, mentor).

Of course, it is sometimes difficult to establish a good working relationship with an individual. If the client is preoccupied, does not want coaching, or is deemed "uncoachable" (e.g., they don't think they need coaching, lack trust or openness, are arrogant or impatient or resistant to feedback, or are unwilling to look inside themselves), the quality of coaching outcomes will suffer (Peterson, 2010). Whether attributable primarily to characteristics of the client or to the impact of an uncoachable client on the coach–client relationship, desired coaching outcomes will be negatively affected in either case. CPs are advised to have a discussion with the client in a personally supportive, empathetic way when the individual's readiness for coaching appears to be low and when, therefore, coaching is unlikely to achieve the desired results. The appropriate thing to do in this case is to recommend postponing coaching until there is a more convenient time for the client. If the CP and client are aligned in this decision, both should meet with the client's manager for a discussion. If all are agreed, sponsors will be notified and coaching discontinued for the time being. Investment in leader coaching is not insignificant for a company, and the CP looking out for the company by declining that particular engagement will be appreciated.

If, however, the client does not want to postpone coaching, yet appears not to have time, focus, or energy for coaching, the CP will work with them to figure out what the client will do to make their development a high priority and get their commitment to dedicate energy and focus to coaching. Assuming that the client and the circumstance are suitable for entering and benefiting from leadership coaching, establishing a strong and effective relationship requires authenticity, candor, and the full commitment of the client in their development journey. As is true for all helping relationships, the more the client feels that the CP genuinely cares about them and their success and fulfillment, the stronger will be the bond of trust between CP and client, enabling the kind of dialogue, introspection, and interactions between them that challenge and often change mindsets and result in the best possible outcomes.

Because attributes of the client and the environment in which they live and work are important factors that affect the success of coaching (Frisch, 2005a, 2005b; Lowman, 2002; Vandaveer et al., 2016), it is important to know as much as possible about the client and their context before beginning coaching. Just a few examples are (a) motivation for coaching and development (e.g., is the client's manager requiring that they get coaching? If so, what is the client's attitude about that?), (b) workload and schedule (e.g., how much time is there to devote to coaching and development?), (c) the nature of the culture in which the client needs to be effective, and (d) the mental model of coaching (i.e., how does the client think about developmental coaching?).

Frisch (2005a, 2005b) used two categories for the main distractions and derailers to coaching: (a) characteristics of the coaching client and (b) characteristics of the sponsoring organization. *Coaching caveats* are five specific things to watch out for under each category (see more in Chapter 6). For the organization, the coach needs to explore any equivocation in the commitment to client development, general organizational upheaval and change, strength of the client–sponsor relationship, politicization and competitiveness within organizational culture, and coaching embedded within a larger leadership development program. The first of these is essentially a start–delay decision (e.g., organizational sponsors are not sure about investing resources in the client's development), as mentioned previously; the other caveats are scalable concerns. The more of them that exist, the more risk there is to developmental progress.

The CP needs to consider a number of things relative to the individual coaching client's readiness for engaging in developmental coaching. Examples include (a) personal challenges for the client or client's family, (b) client resilience and risk tolerance to try new behaviors, (c) client emotional stability or reactivity to feedback, (d) client psychological curiosity and self-insight, and (e) motivation to own behavior change goals and have an internal locus of control. The point behind all these considerations is to ensure the CP is well attuned to the potential challenges in each coaching engagement.

Theoretical Frameworks

Because CPs come from a variety of areas of psychology, as described in Chapter 1, there is a wide range of theoretical frameworks used in coaching that serve as important tools in helping to understand the client and their context (i.e., organization and sociocultural environment in which the client must be effective; Vandaveer et al., 2016).

Of the 342 CPs who participated in the Vandaveer et al. (2016) survey (members of American Psychological Association [APA] and/or Society of Consulting Psychology and/or Society for Industrial and Organizational Psychology), 25% or more cited the following theoretical bases as among those they primarily use:

- leadership theory: 72%
- emotional intelligence theory: 55%
- organizational theory: 51%
- cognitive and cognitive behavioral psychological theory: 47%
- behavioral psychology (behavior change or modification): 45%
- positive psychology and appreciative inquiry: 44%
- subject matter experts' personally based or business experience–based approach: 42%
- pragmatic, problem solving, evidence based, action research based: 40%
- action learning: 37%
- systems theory—including family systems, cybernetic systems: 33%
- control theory—goal setting, feedback, self-regulation, self-efficacy: 33%
- cognitive psychology: 32%
- learning theory and social learning: 29%
- social psychology: 25%
- self as instrument of change: 25%

CPs naturally draw primarily from the theoretical foundations of their graduate degrees, yet there was wide agreement that whatever one's academic foundation, there is much to be learned from other areas of psychology and then applied to coaching. For example, psychologists trained in health service psychology typically need to expand their knowledge and experience in organizational and social psychology, including motivation, organizational dynamics, leadership and management science, and measurement (more about this transition in Chapter 5). A particular challenge for health service psychology is the shift from doing clinical therapy to focusing on leader and executive development. CPs need to understand and work with clients within their business organizational contexts, identifying and focusing on the individual's leadership strengths and opportunities for leveraging them more widely, as well as identifying what needs to be strengthened or changed for even greater effectiveness as leader. The leader's context includes the organization's culture and general financial health, the nature and demands of the client's role (i.e., the nature and substance of a leader's responsibility), performance standards and expectations, the people with whom the client works and interacts with regularly (e.g., direct reports, peer colleagues, manager, board of directors [if top executive], other key stakeholders), and the client's networks. The relevant external context includes the organization's place and general reputation in its industry or sector, standing compared with competitors, relationships with investors if it is a public company, and the geopolitical landscape pertaining to the company's industry.

How a client interprets, interacts with, and responds to those factors plays a significant role in determining their effectiveness and development needs. Applying a therapy model in coaching will not only fall short of executive coaching's potential to help the leader "get to the top of their game" as a leader but will also probably be viewed as too narrow and mental health oriented by sponsors of executive coaching. It may not be easy to change from a "what is wrong or needs fixing" mindset to "what are this person's primary strengths for the target leader roles?"—that is, "What is most right with this person?" "Where does their potential for greatness as a leader lie?" and "What could be further developed—as well as what really needs to change—to get to the next levels of leadership effectiveness?"

Similarly, industrial and organizational (I/O) and other general applied psychologists need training and reorientation toward working one-on-one, drawing on relevant principles of counseling or clinical psychology theory. This often requires a shift from predicting leader effectiveness to helping leaders develop, as well as from consulting and advising to facilitating an individual's learning. This can be a challenging shift for those steeped in rigorous statistical analysis and making recommendations based on the probability of being effective in a target role. I/O psychologists especially need to invest time and effort into deepening their understanding of and skill in individualized work in a helping function in which they are an active part of the client's development. For some I/O psychologists, this is uncomfortable and much too personal. Although they may be comfortable with the science part—collecting and analyzing quantified data from people—a good many I/O psychologists are uncomfortable with the art part of coaching, and it is the art part (coach–client relationship or connectedness) that differentiates adequate from excellent coaching outcomes (Bachkirova, 2016; Boyatzis & McKee, 2005; de Haan, 2008; de Haan et al., 2013; Flaherty, 2010).

Psychologists who are naturally oriented toward serving in a helping relationship will find the transition much easier than those who are much more comfortable with statistical prediction and p values, which, of course, require large samples. This methodology, that is, statistical prediction using large samples, is termed *nomothetic* (i.e., establishing generalizations from large sample statistical analyses and applying them to the individual). *Idiographic* approaches—appropriate for working with an individual— by contrast, involve gathering as much information as possible from the individual to understand them (vs. using statistical "probability" based on large samples of people). *Ipsative* assessment (i.e., a "forced-choice" format such that the respondent must choose between or among specific options—vs. rating options on a numeric scale), in addition to normative, is an example of the nature of tools and processes that are in the realm of counseling and clinical psychology that I/O psychologists typically need to learn and become comfortable with and skilled in using—in addition to the normative (compared with large samples of leaders) individual assessments they may use. Other important skills from counseling—and organization development—include inquiry and facilitation skills that lead to client self-insight and learning. Consulting and I/O psychologists—and clinical and counseling psychologists—need to be knowledgeable about principles of adult learning, development, and growth that have emerged and evolved over decades of research and insights from professional practice (Fosnot & Perry, 2005; Kolb, 2015; Kolb & Boyatzis, 2001).

A working familiarity with a variety of theoretical frameworks and models provides the CP with multiple helpful perspectives from which to understand clients more deeply and multiple approaches to facilitating learning to be maximally helpful and effective. With knowledge and experience using a variety of theoretical models, CPs will discover which ones include concepts and approaches that are the most helpful to them in their work with clients (Peltier, 2010). Research has shown that, in practice, experienced coaches acquire agility in applying and switching among several theoretical models, depending on what is presented by a client. Such "model agility" significantly expands the CP's understanding of the client, thereby enabling a wider range of options relative to the coaching approach and tools (Kauffman & Hodgetts, 2016).

The Vandaveer et al. (2016) study showed that less than a third of survey respondents identified learning theory and social learning as one of the most influential theories or frameworks in their practice, and social psychology was named by only 25%. Because coaching psychology facilitates learning and development in another person, it is important that CPs know as much as possible about how people learn (including themselves)—and how different people learn differently. If the selection of coaching models and other tools is tailored to the client's preferred learning style (Kolb, 2015; Kolb & Boyatzis, 2001), their learning will be much easier and richer than if tools are chosen based on the CP's preferred ways of learning. An example is when the CP's preferred learning style is reflective observation and abstract conceptualization, and the client's preferred learning style is concrete experience and active experimentation (Kolb, 2015; see Figure 3.1 and the section titled Experiential Learning Model). The CP may be inclined to provide the client with books, readings, conceptual drawings and metaphors, and so on, to provide the conceptual big picture relative to the client's development needs. That client will likely dread reading volumes of written material (and it may go unread), and the big-picture conceptualizations may be more useful in treating insomnia than acquiring needed learning.

Likewise, the CP who prefers concrete experience and active experimentation may assign homework to the client that involves diving in and practicing a behavioral or interactional technique for learning. If the client's preferred learning style is reflective observation and assimilating

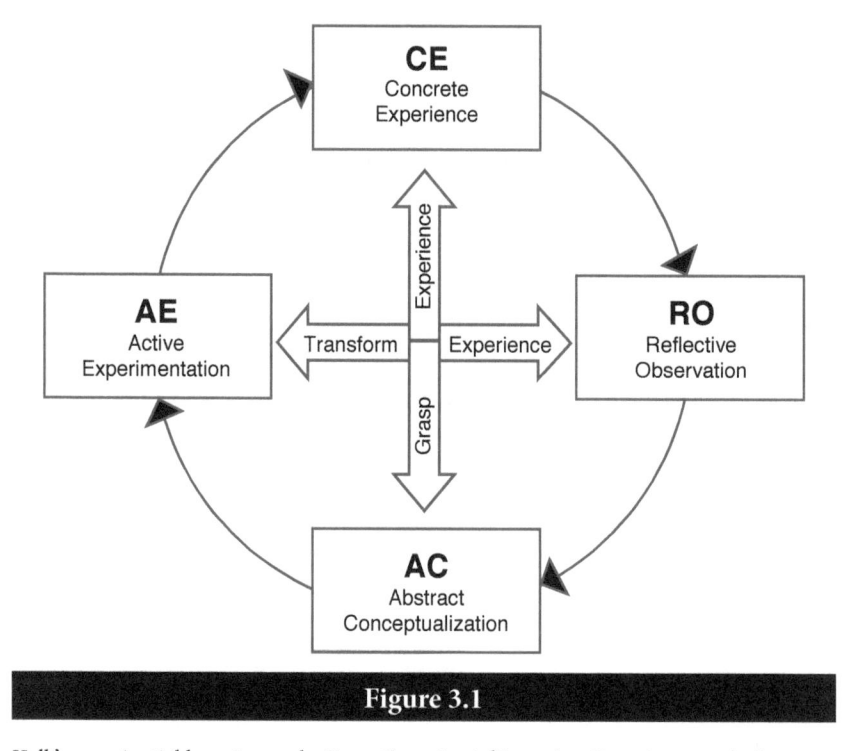

Figure 3.1

Kolb's experiential learning cycle. From *Experiential Learning: Experience as the Source of Learning and Development* (2nd ed., p. 51), by D. A. Kolb, 2015, Pearson Education. Copyright 2015 by Pearson Education. Reprinted with permission.

before active experimentation ("Let me reflect and understand this first"), they will be uncomfortable trying a new behavior before first understanding the rationale, how it will work, what the benefit and potential pitfalls are, how they will be safe, and so on.

Another theoretical model that deserves mention here is one from gestalt theory: dialogical self-theory (Pugh & Broome, 2020), which combines gestalt psychology and experiential learning theory (Kolb, 2015). It emphasizes the importance of active experiential learning in getting real and sustained behavior change. First used in psychodrama more than a hundred years ago, the method engages the "head, heart, and hands," which has been shown to be necessary for real and sustained behavior change (Pugh & Broome, 2020).

Inasmuch as organizations are social systems (De Cremer et al., 2012; Katz & Kahn, 1978), understanding the social-psychological dynamics of the client's organization is fundamental to understanding the environment in which the client needs to be effective, and it contributes to the CP's selection of approach and tools for coaching.

Clinical and counseling psychologists trained in psychoanalysis may apply that lens in their coaching and will readily pick up on the psychodynamics of—and any dysfunction of—the organization's culture. General applied psychologists who have not been trained in psychoanalysis or psychodynamics will get that information in a different way—for example, in dialogue with the client, direct inquiry about the culture, and from key stakeholder feedback (discussed later in this chapter), if used.

We review two practical learning theories here—both key tools in developmental coaching: Kolb's experiential learning theory and model (Kolb, 2015) and the constructivist learning theory and model (Fosnot & Perry, 2005).

Experiential Learning Theory

David Kolb's work in experiential learning theory—building on the work of Kurt Lewin (1951; field theory), John Dewey (1938; functional psychology and pragmatism), and Jean Piaget (1952, 1968; developmental psychology and cognitive development)—has informed learning and development for decades. Kolb (2015) defined *learning* as "the process whereby knowledge is created through the transformation of experience" (pp. 49–51) and as "a continuous process grounded in experience . . . a continual process of adaptation as we experience life" (p. 67; Dewey, 1938; Kolb & Boyatzis, 2001; Piaget, 1952).

Figure 3.1 shows Kolb's experiential learning cycle model, consisting of two "dialectically related modes of grasping experience": concrete experience (CE)—abstract conceptualization (AC)—and reflective observation (RO)—active experimentation (AE). "Knowledge results from the combination of grasping (taking in information) and transforming (interpreting and acting on) that information" (Kolb, 2015, p. 51).

As measured by Kolb's Learning Style Inventory, a preference for learning through CE emphasizes feeling (vs. thinking)—"an intuitive 'artistic' approach as opposed to a systematic scientific approach to problems" (Kolb, 2015, p. 105). An individual with this preference values relating to people and being involved in activities.

A preference for learning through RO means focusing on understanding the meaning of ideas and situations by carefully observing and impartially describing them. These individuals rely on their thoughts and feelings to form opinions and are typically characterized by patience, impartiality, and thoughtful judgment, according to Kolb.

A preference for AC involves using logic, ideas, and concepts and emphasizing thinking (vs. feeling) and building general theories before trying to understand unique specific aspects. These individuals "value precision, the rigor and discipline of analyzing ideas, and aesthetic quality of a neat conceptual system" (Kolb, 2015, p. 105).

A preference for AE emphasizes practical applications as opposed to reflective understanding—a pragmatic concern with what works. Emphasis is on doing versus observing. These individuals are willing to take some risk to achieve objectives, are typically good at getting things done, and value having influence.

Tailoring the approach to coaching according to the client's preferred ways of learning—as well as other considerations—will be much more effective than if the CP approaches coaching in a way more aligned with their own preferred ways of learning.

Kolb's Learning Style Inventory can be used to assess the client's learning style; however, I (VV) have found that most leaders readily identify their style when shown Kolb's diagram and definitions of each style. For the purposes of developmental coaching, that has worked well.

Constructivist Learning Theory

From the constructivist perspective (Fosnot & Perry, 2005), the learner is not a passive recipient of knowledge from another person. Rather, the learner takes an active role in constructing their own understanding. Learning requires the learner to do some cognitive processing in acquiring new knowledge and understanding, which in turn requires that the new information be somehow related to the person's existing knowledge structures. In other words, learning requires being able to hook the new information to something already known through reflection, cogitation, and incorporation of the new information into the existing structure. Thus, learning involves observation, processing and interpretation, and personalizing and incorporating the information into their knowledge base. In addition to the cognitive aspects of learning (Piaget, 1952, 1968), constructivist theory also posits that learning is

- contextual—that is, the information to be learned is in a particular context and taps into the learner's beliefs and conceptions of knowledge (Ernest, 1991);
- a social activity (Dewey, 1938; Vygotsky, 1978)—that is, it arises from social interactions in a learning context; and
- personal—that is, individuals' subjective interpretations of a teaching activity differ, and individuals' takeaways from a learning experience are contextual, including cultural. Thus, different people may take away somewhat different meanings from the same learning experience.

We find both learning theories and models—Kolb's experiential learning and constructivism (Fosnot, 1996)—are useful for understanding how individuals learn in general and determining a client's preferred ways of learning to adapt one's coaching approach accordingly. The CP needs to find ways to relate new information or concepts to the client's experiences, understandings, and beliefs.

Coaching Models

In Chapter 2, we mentioned the value of having a structural framework— that is, a model—to guide the coaching work with the client in Levels 1 to 3 coaching. A coaching model serves as a conceptual road map of the coaching and learning journey and provides clarity about the process of coaching and learning, helping to guide the coaching conversation and keep the client and coach on track toward achieving the coaching goals. Such models are not meant to be rigid or prescriptive. In fact, more than one model can be used in a coaching engagement, as more is learned that indicates the usefulness of another model—or parts of another model. Each model is typically associated with a characteristic question framework that the CP uses to structure the coaching conversation (Stout-Rostron, 2014).

As the primary tool, the CP selects the coaching model that best fits the type of coaching and the CP's skill and comfort in using it. Of the many different coaching models that have been developed, we review here a few of the more well-known and widely used ones, as well as my (VV's) personal model, which is an adaptation and evolution of several other models for use in Level 3 coaching and may be helpful for some Level 4 advisory work. Over time, as the CP builds expertise and a strong experience base, they will evolve their own model of coaching, typically including multiple theoretical and practice models ("model agility"; Frisch et al., 2012; Kauffman & Hodgetts, 2016; Stout-Rostron, 2014) and some combination of parts of existing coaching models plus the CP's unique adaptation.

GROW

John Whitmore's (1992) GROW model is a basic four-stage behavioral and cognitive behavioral goal-setting model that is widely recognized, primarily for its metaphoric acronym (growth, development) and usefulness. GROW stands for goal, reality, options, will. What is the client's goal? What is the client's current reality with respect to the goal? What are the client's options (alternative strategies for achieving the goal)? And what will the client do, given what they have learned? In the last stage, the CP facilitates the client in developing a plan, complete with steps they will take and a timeline for accomplishing the goal or goals.

GROW is an especially popular model for use in Level 1 and Level 2 coaching, and it is often used as well in Level 3 engagements in which the approach is typically behavioral or cognitive behavioral goal setting. Many CPs use GROW as part of applying a cognitive behavioral approach.

CLEAR

CLEAR is a five-stage cognitive behavioral model developed by Peter Hawkins in the early 1980s, preceding the GROW model (see Hawkins's

2012 book, *Creating a Coaching Culture*). The acronym stands for contracting, listening, exploring, action, and review. *Contracting* here has the same meaning as described in Chapter 2—that is, it means agreeing on the preliminary goals, process, ground rules, and so on. Clear and active listening requires that the CP consciously focuses on what the client says—and on what they don't say that may be conveying or suggesting meaning—taking note of both verbal and nonverbal behaviors, working to identify underlying assumptions, and asking clarifying questions to check the CP's understanding and interpretations. Like options in the GROW model, exploring in the CLEAR model refers to looking at options through a process of helping the client reflect on how their present state relative to their goal is impacting them, then using that information to generate and evaluate options for actions they might take to make progress. The CP facilitates the client's thinking and working through the various options and deciding on the best way forward, followed by developing and implementing a developmental action plan. The final stage of CLEAR is review, which involves reflection on what worked, what didn't work, and what the client will do to sustain the positive changes. We see this as a particularly important step, and of course, it can easily be added to GROW (GROW-R).

The following models are especially useful for Level 3 coaching for leader development in a current role or for preparation of a leader to move into roles that are different or at a higher level of management. They can also be used for developing identified high-potential leaders. Facilitating learning at this level of coaching typically entails collaborating with the client in clarifying goals and how success will be measured; examining what the client has done to date in pursuit of those goals, including what progress has been made and what difficulties have been experienced; and identifying what will be required to achieve the goals. A cognitive behavioral approach is typically used, reviewing what has been done and what needs to be done to achieve the goal, as well as examining the client's thinking and beliefs that the client has about themselves that may be self-limiting—or effective in facilitating progress. Sometimes work is at the subconscious level of awareness, facilitating the client's thinking, reflecting, and helping to spark key insights that catalyze changes in mindset that facilitate progress toward the goal.

Nested Levels Model of Coaching

Pamela Weiss (2019) referred to two common approaches to coaching: (a) "I am expert. Let me fix you," and (b) "You are perfect and whole and have all the answers within yourself." The underlying assumption of the first is, of course, "I know, and you don't."

Weiss (2019) pointed out that the second approach is partially true in that people do have answers within themselves, and the job of the coach is to "evoke it." She also noted that people have blind spots, and skillful coaching can illuminate and help uncover them. Coaching is not about providing expertise. It is about developing human beings. It is about helping the person learn and grow. As coaches, our job is to leave our clients better off without us.

Weiss (2019) referred to coaching characterized by the coach helping the client become better, faster, more efficient, and so on, at accomplishing their tasks and getting their work done as *horizontal* coaching. This type of coaching consists of, for example, helping clients to "clarify their goals, laying out a set of action steps to move them toward those goals, and then setting up structures to ensure that they stay on track" (Weiss, 2019, para. 11). This is a behaviorist approach.

The obvious problem with this approach is that it is short term. When you remove the stimulus, the behavior snaps right back to the "norm." It may work for a while, but it rarely sticks (Weiss, 2019).

Weiss (2019) described *vertical* coaching as that which helps the client with deeper learning and a greater likelihood of real change in developing and strengthening competence. Weiss identified three vertical "nested levels" of coaching. Her description of the coach's role is as follows:

> Our task as coaches is to help . . . our clients to [see] new possibilities and potential; inviting them to see and inhabit more of the sky. A coaching relationship is where the coach sheds light on the client's

"blind spots," challenging and stretching their fixed views of them-selves, others, and the world. This is work that none of us can do alone. It's only together that we can expand our sky. (Weiss, 2019, last para.)

Integrative Model

Jonathan Passmore's (2007) integrative model of coaching (see Figure 3.2) is probably the most comprehensive published coaching model for the leader and those who provide executive coaching, representing work at multiple levels (behavioral, cognitive, and subconscious), within the context of an effective coach–client partnership. Passmore described the primary objective of executive coaching as facilitating "performance-enhancing behavioral change within the workplace" (p. 69). His model features six "streams" that work together:

- developing the coaching partnership
- maintaining the coaching partnership
- focusing on behavior change, achieved through "deepening the coachee's problem-solving and planning skills" (Passmore, 2007, p. 70)
- deepening the client's understanding of the relationship between their thoughts and behavior (*conscious cognition*)
- focusing on the cognitive processes that are outside of conscious aware-ness by working to deepen self-awareness and insight to bring into conscious awareness aspects of thought, motivation, deeply ingrained assumptions, and so on, that are serving to inhibit or overly limit effec-tive performance (*unconscious cognition*)
- attending to the cultural context in which both coachee and coach operate—and within which the coachee must be effective

Familiarity with several science- and practice-based models (see Stout-Rostron, 2014, for a review of many more models) will help beginning CPs as they gain experience. Eventually, the CP will naturally gravitate to one or several models that they find most useful. Ultimately, the CP will probably evolve their preferred model of coaching, as encouraged by several models' authors, including Passmore (2007).

My (VV's) personal model, the integrative contextual learning model (see Figures 3.3. 3.4, and 3.5), is an adaptation of Passmore's (2007)

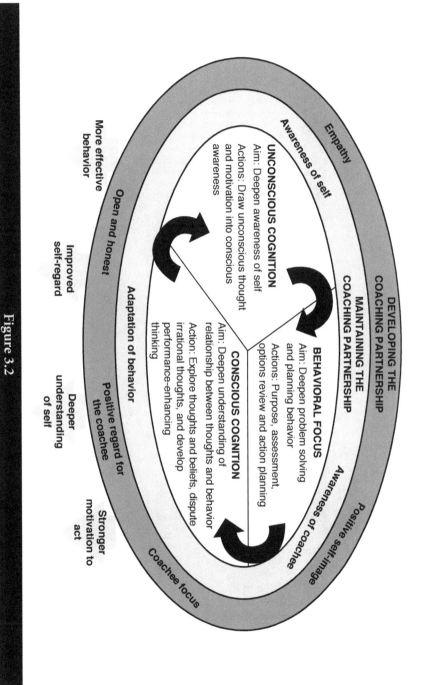

Figure 3.2

Passmore's integrative model of coaching. Adapted from "An Integrative Model for Executive Coaching," by J. Passmore, 2007, *Consulting Psychology Journal*, 59(1), p. 69 (https://doi.org/10.1037/1065-9293.59.1.68). Copyright 2007 by the American Psychological Association.

COACHING PROCESS STAGES
(Nested Recursive Levels)
PROCESS METHODS & DEPTH

Horizontal →
Vertical ↓

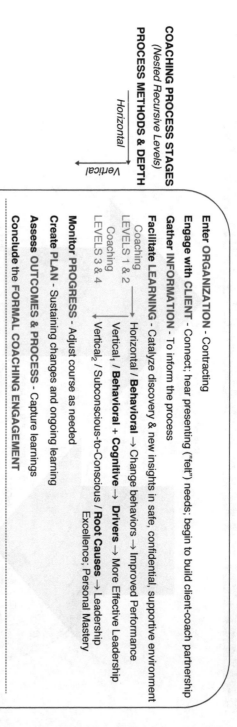

Enter ORGANIZATION - Contracting

Engage with CLIENT - Connect; hear presenting ("felt") needs; begin to build client-coach partnership

Gather INFORMATION - To inform the process

Facilitate LEARNING - Catalyze discovery & new insights in safe, confidential, supportive environment

Coaching
LEVELS 1 & 2 ——→ Horizontal / **Behavioral** → Change behaviors → Improved Performance

Coaching
LEVELS 3 & 4 ——→ Vertical$_1$ / **Behavioral** + **Cognitive** → **Drivers** → More Effective Leadership

Vertical$_2$ / Subconscious-to-Conscious / **Root Causes** → Leadership Excellence; Personal Mastery

Monitor PROGRESS - Adjust course as needed

Create PLAN - Sustaining changes and ongoing learning

Assess OUTCOMES & PROCESS - Capture learnings

Conclude the FORMAL COACHING ENGAGEMENT

Capture NEW INSIGHTS, LEARNINGS → Incorporate learnings → Equip self

Figure 3.3

Integrated, contextual, learning model of coaching.

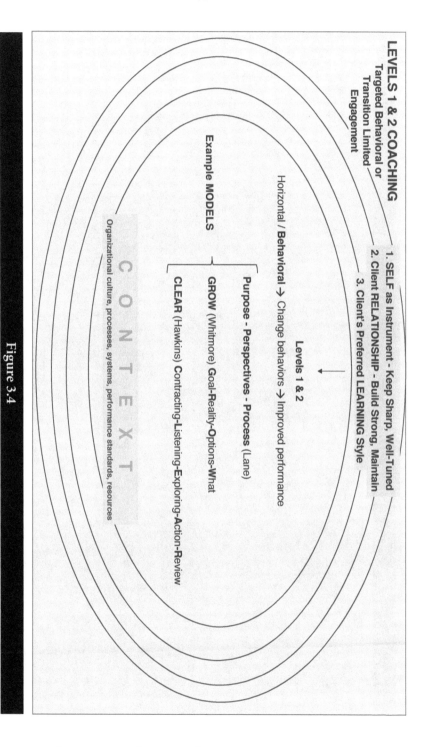

LEVELS 1 & 2 COACHING
Targeted Behavioral or
Transition Limited
Engagement

1. SELF as Instrument - Keep Sharp, Well-Tuned

2. Client RELATIONSHIP - Build Strong, Maintain

3. Client's Preferred LEARNING Style

Horizontal / **Behavioral** → Change behaviors → Improved performance

Levels 1 & 2

Example **MODELS**

Purpose - Perspectives - Process (Lane)

GROW (Whitmore) Goal-Reality-**O**ptions-What

CLEAR (Hawkins) Contracting-Listening-Exploring-Action-Review

C O N T E X T
Organizational culture, processes, systems, performance standards, resources

Figure 3.4

Integrative, contextual, learning model of coaching. Level 1: behavioral.

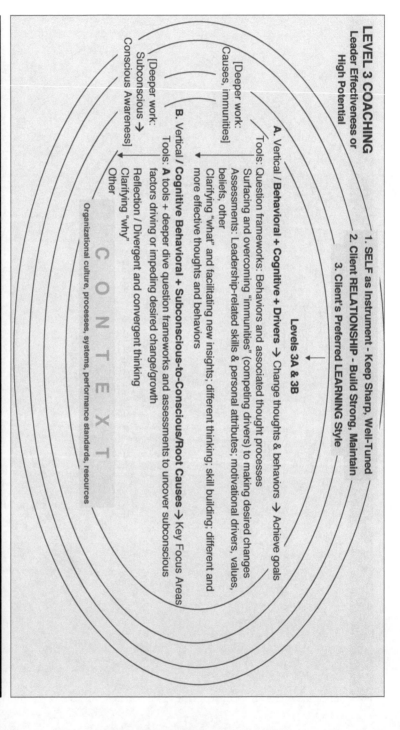

Figure 3.5

Integrative, contextual, learning model of coaching—cognitive behavioral and subconscious-to-conscious: root causes.

integrative model and includes features of Weiss's (2019) nested levels model, plus two additional important elements: (a) organizational culture and context and (b) the client's learning style preference. The context, including the culture, within which the client must be effective and within which coach and client are working, is inextricably a key factor in what is required for effectiveness in the client's organizational role. Passmore accounts for organizational culture, although it is not represented in the diagram of his model, and his model effectively represents levels of coaching (behavioral, conscious cognition, and unconscious cognition), referred to by Weiss (2019) as "nested levels."

Identifying the client's preferred learning style and adapting coaching to that style make it much easier for the client to learn and grow.

Figure 3.3 shows an overview of the model. According to Weiss (2019), levels of complexity of coaching work move from "what" (doing), to "how" (learning), to "who." Our coaching complexity continuum (see Table 1.1) distinguishes four levels of coaching complexity—from limited short-term behavior-focused coaching to more in-depth cognitive behavioral coaching at the conscious cognition and unconscious cognition levels, as in Passmore's (2007) integrative model. As shown in Vandaveer's integrative, contextual learning model (Figure 3.5), the process in Level 3 coaching is integrative in that it moves among behavioral, cognitive, and subconscious-to-conscious learning and awareness. The process is recursive in that the learnings and insights from each phase inform the next and make insights from prior steps clearer. Learning is continual for both client and coach.

Figures 3.4 and 3.5 provide closer looks at coaching at different levels of complexity: Levels 1 and 2 in Figure 3.4 and Levels 3 and 4 in Figure 3.5.

Using the integrative, contextual learning model is straightforward. Begin with the outer bands working toward the center of the diagram:

1. Prepare oneself as the primary instrument for facilitating learning in another person.

2. Build and maintain a strong, effective partnership relationship with the client. The CP will likely need to spend plenty of time at the beginning to (a) learn all they can about the client from the client's

perspective—that is, who they are, what their role is in the organiza-tion, what they feel they do best, what they hope to get from coaching, how they conceptualize coaching, and so on—actively discussing and jointly determining what an effective coaching partnership will look like and (b) demonstrate genuine respect and caring about the client to help lay the foundation for a good working relationship.

3. Determine the client's preferred learning style either by a learning-style assessment inventory or by simply asking the client their preferred ways of learning. Engaging in conversation about Kolb's (2015) four identified primary styles, showing the client Kolb's model, will yield insight into how the individual likes and doesn't like to learn. If the client self-identifies as preferring AC and RO, providing conceptual overviews, diagrams, readings, and so on will be much more comfort-able for the client than assigning a homework task of trying out a new behavior or experimenting with doing something different than what they are currently doing (AE). They will want first to understand why and what the purpose is, what is supposed to happen, and what the big picture is.

4. Begin coaching by facilitating the client's learning, as described in the center of the ellipse.

As illustrated in Figure 3.5, coaching may be primarily at the behav-ioral and cognitive behavioral level of conscious awareness ("A" in the Level 3 diagram), or work may also be at deeper levels of conscious-ness, bringing subconscious factors that drive thoughts and behaviors into conscious awareness. This work is where new insights originate, as the coaching process identifies blind spots and uncovers them, and it helps connect different things the individual already knows in new ways that catalyze fresh thinking and different understanding and perspectives.

Developing One's Personal Model of Coaching

The process of evolving one's personal model of coaching will naturally occur as the CP becomes familiar with and skilled in using some of the good models available. Frisch et al. (2012) described a thorough process for drafting and refining each coach's personal model of coaching based on lists of self-reflective questions that focus on three input domains of what the beginning coach brings to the practice (i.e., as a person, an organizational actor, and a learner about coaching) and three output domains (i.e., emerging coaching approach, building a sustainable practice, and ongoing growth as a coach). As described in more detail in Chapter 5 of this book, this conception of a personal model aims to give beginning coaches practical guidelines for becoming professional coaches.

Developing expertise mastery as a CP requires self-reflection, "a modicum of ability, a lot of motivation, timely and expert teaching and coaching for themselves, and approximately 10 years of dedicated, directed practice" (Kilburg, 2016, p. 185). One's natural strengths as a CP in terms of knowledge, skills, personal attributes, motivation, aspirations to help others, curiosity about oneself and others, and drive to be a lifelong learner fuel the CP's constant drive to expand their repertoire of coaching skills and types of clients served. This effort can pay off in becoming a master CP (Vandaveer & Palmer, 2016). This book is aimed at supporting those efforts.

For excellent overviews of more than a dozen of the more well-known coaching models, see Stout-Rostron (2014) and Hernez-Broome and Boyce (2011).

METHODS

Coaching Meetings and the Coaching Conversation

The coaching meeting is, of course, the tool that most people think of when the topic of executive coaching arises. Meetings between coach and client generally occur every week or two, and they are where the active work between CP and client takes place. Coaching meetings involve the use of different tools and techniques, according to (a) the level of coaching, (b) the stage of the coaching engagement, and (c) the particular focus of learning.

The focus of all early coaching meetings consists primarily of (a) relationship building between the CP and client and establishing a strong working alliance; (b) mutual learning and joint meaning making as the

CP works to understand the client and their needs, aspirations, best learning style, and mental models of leadership and coaching and as the client works to understand the coaching–learning–development process and how to maximize the value of the opportunity for working with a professional CP; and (c) identification of preliminary developmental coaching goals.

In Level 1 coaching, the few meetings are behaviorally focused and may yield a draft development plan. In Level 2 coaching, meetings focus on producing a transition plan and supporting the client in productively starting a new role. Level 3 coaching typically involves a process of discovery (e.g., of the client's present state relative to leadership effectiveness, primary strengths, the key areas for focus in coaching, and clarification of the goal or desired state by the conclusion of the coaching engagement), as well as preparation of a leader-development plan. All these types of leadership one-on-one consultations entail both the relevant science pertaining to leading and coaching and the art of effective application.

As the primary tool for facilitating learning and change, the CP determines the most appropriate learning methods, content, tools, and engagement style that will work best with each client for achieving the coaching goals.

It may seem obvious, but it is worth emphasizing that coaching meetings need quiet, privacy, and freedom from distractions. In-person meetings are usually in the client's office or a conference room. Many CPs prefer a neutral, less busy conference room free from distractions, and they request that the client reserve such a space. Video conference meetings are increasingly common and can work well. As many have experienced during the global pandemic that is affecting almost everyone worldwide at this writing, various video conference platforms have proven their value and utility. Meetings by telephone can work well if the client does no multitasking. Although CPs want to cultivate a friendly and comfortable tone with clients, meeting at restaurants or coffee shops is not recommended because those settings are not adequately private. CPs should do their best to schedule coaching meetings at times and in places that support freedom of inquiry and expression and eschew anything that might compromise that.

Another key point about coaching meetings is that if they do not happen, momentum is broken, and development is delayed or ceases. Coaching meetings that are frequently postponed because of client work pressures or competing commitments delay or derail progress on the coaching engagement arc. If coaching meetings are expected to happen every 2 weeks, missing a meeting may mean the CP and client have no contact for 3 to 4 weeks. That results in a significant loss of momentum. The sacrosanct priority of coaching meetings needs to be modeled by the CP and conveyed as an expectation to the client. As discussed in Chapter 2, contracting must include the importance of keeping coaching appointments. If postponements by the client are frequent, the CP and client need to explore the reasons, the client's motivation, and ways to get back on track. Of course, each CP has an individual capacity for work, details, and time pressure, but coaching requires an attentiveness that is unlike other types of consulting. If clients do not feel the CP's attentiveness and commitment, the foundational relationship between coach and client will be compromised.

Careful preparation for each coaching meeting is important. The particular coaching model used guides the agenda. For example, GROW begins with goal setting, followed by realities (the current situation), and so on.

Although a general structure is always helpful for staying on track toward the goals, in Level 3 coaching, a significant value of coaching is spontaneity and flexibility. Coaching should support clients and CPs going in new directions, as well as revisiting previous topics, all in the service of extending client insight and connecting with their motivation for learning and growth. As several of the tools and techniques described in this chapter imply, coaches can follow their intuition to inquire deeply, listen with one's whole self, apply multiple psychological perspectives to understand a client's dilemmas better, reframe client statements to open up possibilities, or suggest a role-play with the client to try out a new behavior. As with other guidelines, session structure should support freedom in the engagement to go in new and exciting directions. Structure too rigidly followed will diminish the creative aspects of coaching.

A final closure meeting with the client's manager and, if appropriate, other sponsors will include a look back at the learning generated by the coaching engagement, celebration of the client's progress, and planning for ongoing learning, supported by the client's manager. The closure meeting for the CP and client is an essential wrap-up of the engagement. Goals and progress are reviewed and extrapolated into the near future with the CP's commitment to continue learning as planned, including the acquisition of ongoing feedback. The CP and client must prepare for the final coaching meeting and the effects that separation might have on each of them. Although final coaching meetings are positive and celebratory, the CP must also be prepared for and acknowledge the likelihood of experiencing sadness, a natural response to concluding a meaningful coach–client relationship.

It is also effective practice for the CP to request feedback from the client about the coaching process. Although sponsoring organizations themselves are likely to conduct a more formal review (see Chapter 4), CPs can ask for feedback in the moment or as a soon-to-follow brief survey. All professionals need feedback on their services to grow and improve as they work toward expertise mastery.

Goal Setting and Measures of Progress

Whatever theoretical models coaches prefer for understanding clients (described earlier), almost all coaching engagements involve setting tangible goals and criteria for assessing progress, supported by a series of action steps to help the client move toward those goals. As an important part of the development plan, achieving these targets reflects important milestones in the coaching process (see Chapter 2). Having a written plan, even if it continues to evolve and change, is both a method of helping the client change and a deliverable of the coaching engagement. A written development plan includes the goals and the specific, tailored actions needed to achieve them; they are essential reminders to the client about changes they have committed to making. The plan is a deliverable because it is the main way that coaching sponsors can see what coach and client have targeted to work on, and it invites those sponsors to reengage with the client in their natural roles to directly support the client's development. For all these reasons, a written development plan for clients is a foundational element of their learning and development journey.

A key challenge in developing new and/or strengthening leadership skills—and/or changing managerial and leadership behaviors—is the effort required to set up feedback loops so behavior can continue to improve. Behavioral observations are soft but important data because they represent others' perceptions of the leader's actions (i.e., their perceived and felt impact). Although a leader's effectiveness impacts the organization's performance, there is no direct hard measurement; identifying the leader's contribution to business results among myriad other factors is impossible. Key stakeholders' perceptual feedback is helpful, and often CPs plan for a "Time 1 and Time 2" process of collecting feedback. If that is not done, it can be difficult to arrange after the formal coaching engagement. Given these challenges to assessing ongoing development, goals and actions and how progress will be determined on a development plan are an important part of maintaining the client's momentum and ongoing development. Client sharing of development plans with sponsors and other colleagues, however clients prefer to do that, is an important step in creating proximal feedback loops for ongoing client learning.

An important part of the CP's responsibility is helping the client continue to assume full responsibility for their ongoing development, as well as helping them erect mechanisms for ongoing receipt of valuable feedback. This also allows the CP to move toward closure of the engagement with greater confidence that the client is set up to continue making progress. In effect, development plans are concrete ways to connect the client's development work within the organization's established processes for development, performance evaluation, identification of leadership potential, succession planning, and so on. Key values in coaching include leaving both the client and the system much better than at the beginning and, in each engagement, working toward a natural and effective conclusion of the coaching engagement.

Chapter 4 reviews research on the effectiveness of coaching that uses these methods. Although proximal feedback is always more useful to clients than distal feedback from an evaluation study, such studies are essential to add to the research foundation of coaching and bring science-based insights to the practice.

Assessments

For all applied areas of psychology, assessment is a fundamental aspect of effective practice and science. With respect to coaching psychology, assessment skills needed are at all three levels of consulting psychology: individual, group, and organizational (Silzer et al., 2018). Because executive coaching must consider the client in context, it is necessary to understand as much as possible about the coaching client's organization (Katz & Kahn, 1978; Turner, 2007; Winum et al., 2002). Although practical considerations (e.g., project scope, time constraints, budget) put limits on the nature and extent of organizational assessment that can be conducted, individual assessment of the coaching client is a key tool for CPs, and an understanding of the organizational context will need to be acquired through interviews with the coaching client, their manager, other coaching sponsors, and other key stakeholders (e.g., in 360-degree interviews for the coaching client).

In coaching psychology, assessment tools include both qualitative (descriptive) and standardized (scorable and normed) assessments. The primary assessment tools used in executive coaching are (a) interview, (b) dialogue with the client and client's manager, (c) feedback from key stakeholders (360-degree-feedback interviews or surveys), (d) psychological assessment inventories and tests, (e) existing performance reviews and other information that the client believes to be pertinent, and (f) observations of the client in coaching meetings and other on-the-job venues. A must-read first book for those planning to use individual psychological assessment in the selection and development of leaders is the classic *Individual Psychological Assessment* (Jeanneret & Silzer, 1998; see also Vandaveer et al., 2019, 2020).

Interviews of Clients and Sponsors

The interview is an essential method for gathering important data to inform the coaching process. It is used by all CPs for a variety of purposes and in different formats. Examples include the following:

- preliminary interviews with the contact client, primary client, and that person's manager and talent management (TM) professional for the purposes of learning about the coaching services needed and related information (e.g., about the potential coaching client, their position in the company, what management's expectations are, nature of the context and culture);
- the subsequent preliminary interview with the potential coaching client also for gathering information for the purpose of determining the degree of match between what the client needs and wants and the CP's capabilities of fulfilling those needs; and
- once a CP is engaged to provide coaching, an initial assessment interview of the client, often conducted for the purpose of becoming acquainted, learning about the person's role, context, background, preliminary coaching goals, aspirations, concerns, preferred learning style, and so on for the important purpose of beginning to build trust and a strong, effective working alliance with the client.

It should be noted that not all CPs use an initial assessment interview. Some prefer to dive into coaching and learn what they need to know through dialogue along the way. In the study conducted by Vandaveer et al. (2016), 86% of the survey participants said that they did initial interviews with coaching clients.

Developing effective interviewing and dialogic skills is essential to effective coaching. CPs need to obtain good training in skillful interviewing. Although many people see themselves as effective at interviewing, there is much more to it than meets the eye, particularly with respect to assessment interviewing (Jeanneret & Silzer, 1998), such as that used in coaching psychology. One of the most important aspects of skillful interviewing and dialogue is deep listening—and hearing—that is, hearing and really understanding what the client means and connecting with it.

Early interview-based interactions with clients are also useful in exploring the client's understanding and preferences about the coaching process, beliefs about leadership development, and general preferred learning style. CPs also ask about the client's organizational context, job, constituencies, and competitors (both internal and external). It is helpful for the CP to get early indications of the client's comfort with and skill in introspection and self-reflection, flexibility in considering others' perspectives, and readiness for learning through coaching. Coaching takes commitment, as well as a supportive context, and the interview can explore the client's energy and time available for the coaching process. Confidential interviews of key stakeholders (i.e., 360-degree feedback), which gather information about how people who work most closely with the individual perceive them in their leader role, are particularly valuable for both the client and CP in learning about the context and receiving valuable feedback for the coaching client to consider in developing the coaching goals.

It is important to note that the preliminary coaching interview is different from the clinical or counseling intake interview. Although some clinically trained CPs may blend the two, many CPs (42%–44% of subject matter experts in the study by Vandaveer et al., 2016) draw more from positive psychology in that it is focused on understanding the client's achievements, aspirations, strengths, and values (their platform for greatness). Areas for development are explored relative to helping the client achieve the next levels of effectiveness in their leader role and their career aspirations. In short, the interview for leader coaching is focused on the present—aspirations, needs, challenges, and professional development—not on deep-seated emotional problems or internal conflict dynamics (the realm of clinical therapy). To the extent that psychological or emotional obstacles appear during coaching, coach and client can explore how much these are likely to impede the client's ability to profit from the coaching. Most often, CPs fold these insights into understanding the client and shaping coaching interventions appropriately. In rare circumstances, it may be advisable for the client to get additional support from a counseling or clinical psychologist to resolve emotional disturbances affecting the client's functioning.

The specific coaching model used will guide the coach's approach to interviewing. Thus, those CPs who use a cognitive behavioral model in their coaching will seek to understand the client's cognitive framework or the mental (cognitive and emotional) structures of interpretation used in making decisions (Palmer & Whybrow, 2008; White, 2006) and/or that drive their behavior. Occasionally, a cognitive interview may be used to help clients recall the details of formative situations that resulted in learning that became part of their mindset and usual behavior. The cognitive interview can help clients realize that past learning may have outlived its usefulness or may simply not apply in their current context—or that past learning is interfering with present learning.

A cognitive behavioral model is useful in understanding how the client arrived at important decisions, what beliefs and guiding principles they applied, and what their aspirations are. Depending on the CP's interview style and skill, the client's emotions and emotional self-regulation can be important topics to explore, such as their aspirations, passions, and attitudes toward challenges (e.g., tendencies toward optimism, pessimism, or neutral feelings [low affect]), as well as their frustrations, fears, negative self-judgment and self-defeating thoughts, or anger triggers. In these ways, a cognitive behavioral approach to interviewing can facilitate a deeper exploration of the client's life and career experiences—and "what they are made of" that feeds into the development of their unique best leader self. I/O psychologists can benefit from learning from their clinical and counseling colleagues in honing these skills toward helping clients improve and grow.

I/O psychologists are typically trained to conduct behavioral structured interviews. These have application in Level 1 coaching (described in Chapter 1) when helping clients understand their 360-degree feedback or assessment profiles from standardized assessments. Even though they are time limited, the interview of the client in preparation for their receiving their 360-degree feedback has multiple purposes: (a) to become acquainted with the client's goals and context; (b) to review the results of assessments and, through dialogue, jointly interpret the results; (c) to explore the client's reactions to taking the assessments and the results, using that information to understand even better; and (d) to facilitate dialogue with the client about the results and possible actions to take toward growth and development, leveraging strengths and identifying one or more key focus areas for development. It is important that the CP's interview and dialogue style during these feedback sessions is supportive of the client, even in brief coaching, helping them process the feedback in a realistic and constructive way and create a development action plan.

Whatever the model or level of coaching engagement, conducting interviews and engaging in dialogue with the client with a high level of skill and facility for purposeful impact is an essential competency for CPs. Training and continual improvement in the application of interviewing in coaching are highly recommended. Although interview training is beyond the scope of this book, there are many useful resources the CP can consult (Garman, 2002; Jeanneret & Silzer, 1998; Miller & Rollnick, 2002; Peltier, 2010, pp. 13–15; Stoltzfus, 2008).

Stakeholder Feedback (Both Qualitative and Scorable 360-Degree Feedback)

A useful tool that has been mentioned several times thus far for helping the coaching client enhance self-insight and awareness of the impact on others is feedback from key stakeholders (i.e., the client's manager, peer colleagues, direct reports, others) collected through confidential interviews by the coach or through a 360-degree survey. In the Vandaveer et al. (2016) study of foundational competency in coaching, 51% of respondents to the practice analysis survey indicated that they use a "multisource feedback survey" in 66% to more than 90% of coaching engagements. When a survey is used, there are many standardized questionnaires to choose from, and organizations sometimes add customized questions. Surveys are sent to the client and stakeholders (e.g., manager, direct reports, peers) so that confidential, comprehensive feedback can be collected. To ensure anonymity (except for manager feedback) and encourage candid feedback, organizations using such tools often outsource the administration and compiling of the feedback results, which may be used in coaching as well as other programs for leadership development.

In a meta-analysis of studies on this assessment method, Jones et al. (2016) found no benefit from 360-degree feedback surveys in coaching contexts. The 360-degree feedback interview has many advantages over the standardized survey, such as greater precision in capturing the stakeholders' actual perceptions because of the opportunity to dialogue and the ability to get a more complete response. Although the interview-based feedback is more labor-intensive than a 360-degree survey—and therefore a greater financial investment for the client organization—there are several important reasons for its major appeal to clients and CPs alike:

- Respondents report preferring to have a conversation with the CP rather than responding to a questionnaire. They can express themselves more clearly and provide detail about the client's leadership behaviors that may be difficult to align with preset scorable items. The interview method also allows for observations and perspectives that survey questions may not have anticipated. Respondents appreciate that their direct observations and perceptions are captured and summarized by an experienced professional purely for developmental purposes.

- Clients appreciate the rigor of the process and the level of detail that CPs can bring into the feedback. Having conducted eight to 15 interviews from multiple perspectives, the CP is well informed about how the client is perceived. The CP can be an invaluable partner with the client in analyzing perceived strengths and identifying key focus areas for development grounded in behavioral examples. This also enables the CP to brainstorm knowledgeably with the client about goals, strategies, and action ideas for well-founded development planning.

- Even though 360-degree surveys often have space for open-ended comments, the use of those is inconsistent. It may be the case that respondents who have the most direct observation of the client have the least time to write in responses. Therefore, write-in comments may be a skewed sample of observations of the client and yet carry more weight than deserved. This is another reason that even in short engagements partnering with a skilled CP to interpret 360-degree survey results is recommended. Using interview-based input about a client avoids issues with write-in comments on surveys.

Stakeholder 360-degree feedback interviews during coaching Level 3 typically include eight to 15 colleagues, are 30 to (more typically) 60 minutes long, and are conducted in person or by video conference or phone, depending on scheduling preferences and the level of the respondent.

The interview will be much more productive and informative if the key stakeholder being interviewed knows ahead of time the kinds of topics the coach would like to discuss so they can come to the meeting prepared. Providing the general topic areas but also emphasizing that the interview will not be limited to those because the CP seeks to understand how the individual truly sees the client is helpful.

Although anonymity of input is assured with peers and direct reports, the input from the client's manager and possibly from other senior managers is typically not reported anonymously—with that respondent's permission.

Of course, any assessment has potential pitfalls, and it is important to be aware of them at the outset and take steps to minimize or prevent them. With respect to the 360-degree stakeholder feedback interview, common pitfalls include (a) a nonrepresentative sample of interviewees, causing the results to be skewed to the positive or negative; (b) the respondents' reluctance to provide candid feedback; and (c) transference or countertransference between the CP and interviewee. With respect to (a), it is rarely the case (but it does happen) that the coaching client selects the key stakeholders to be interviewed, and only those that the client knows will give them strongly positive feedback. That has happened in some prestigious organizations in which competition for upward advancement was particularly competitive and/or the culture was characterized by low trust or intimidation (these are just a couple of examples among many scenarios). It is important that the key stakeholders selected to participate be selected by both the coaching client, their boss, and, when appropriate, the human resources (HR) or TM representative responsible for leader development to ensure a representative sample of perspectives.

With regard to (b)—feedback participants' reluctance to provide candid feedback—for whatever reason, a highly skilled CP who has earned the trust of everyone—even people who do not fully trust each other— can usually obtain valuable information by putting safeguards in place to ensure the anonymity of individuals' responses. Of course, the participant needs to feel "safe." When the organization's culture is characterized by low trust and fear, the skilled CP can get back to the participants before delivering the feedback to the coaching client and share with them how their input will be worded to ensure the anonymity of their responses. (Note that in many years of my [VV's] collecting 360-degree feedback in this way for clients, this situation has happened only twice, and both times resulted in positive outcomes for the coaching client and the organization.)

Pitfall (c), transference and countertransference, refers to the dynamic between the CP and an interviewee. It is probably a rare occurrence (we have not experienced this to our knowledge), but if either the CP or the interviewee reminds the other of someone they have strong emotions about, it could potentially impact the feedback provided (or interpreted). The highly skilled CP will pick up on that (especially one who is clinically trained) and, once aware of it, can usually counteract the effects in the interview. I/O psychologists and other general applied psychologists who have no clinical training may be oblivious to this dynamic and not recognize the impact on the feedback provided. However, as we recommend in Chapter 5, everyone coming out of any graduate psychology program needs to acquire knowledge and skills from other psychology disciplines—and from management science—to be satisfactorily prepared to provide coaching services.

I/O and consulting psychologists are familiar with content-analysis processes when interpreting qualitative feedback, and these can be applied directly to interview data. The CP similarly extracts key strengths, development needs, and possibly other themes from across the interviews, providing appropriate examples as long as the source's identity is protected. If useful to specific clients, respondent categories (e.g., peer, direct report) with three or more individuals in each group can be used to divide the feedback themes.

The summarized themes are typically written by the coach in a report that is comprehensive, is maximally "receivable" by the client, and protects the anonymity of specific responders. Depending on the degree of the client's self-insight, as revealed in coaching meeting conversations before this step in the process (see Chapter 2), clients often anticipate key themes. Nonetheless, having those confirmed by the coach's rigorous interview process is a valuable tool that, when skillfully used by the CP, is typically a powerful motivator toward the client's development, and any new insights that emerge are highly valued. Often, the client is pleasantly surprised at the nature and extent of positive perceptions of the stakeholders, and often, one or more blind spots about how the client can be more effective are also revealed.

It is also the case that many clients take their strengths for granted, and this process allows for the appropriate acknowledgment of ways that others value the client, and it can offer encouragement to recognize and even more fully leverage one's strengths. Generally, both strengths and development themes from the summary report carry directly, with appropriate wording and action commitments, to the client's development plan. Thus, the stakeholder feedback provides important information that will be reviewed (at a high level) and approved by the client's manager and shared with other coaching sponsors, so everyone can be on board and support the individual's leader development work. Although the comprehensive feedback summary is typically confidential and for the client only, in many cases, a summary report is jointly prepared for the manager by the CP and client that highlights the consensus areas of strengths and the key focus areas for development based on stakeholders' perceptions.

In some cases, in the contracting phase of the coaching engagement, it is agreed that the client's manager will see the 360-degree feedback report. If that is the case, participants need to know before they respond.

Standardized Assessment Inventories

Standardized assessment inventories, properly used, can be helpful tools in coaching for better understanding the client (e.g., motivational drivers, values, needs, personality characteristics, preferred leadership styles, emotional intelligence), including helping to understand better others' perceptions of the client as obtained in 360-degree feedback (Lowman, 2021). The assessment tools most useful for individual leader coaching identify attributes and motivational drivers that are the most relevant to leading effectively in one's organization. Next are some examples of leader assessments, with several highlighted that are most frequently used by CPs in coaching. In addition, Chapter 10 in *Advancing Executive Coaching* (Hernez-Broome & Boyce, 2011) has a comprehensive annotated review of assessments frequently used in coaching.

Executive assessment can be defined as "a process of measuring a person's knowledge, skills, abilities, and personal style to evaluate characteristics and behavior that are relevant to (predictive of) successful job performance" (Jeanneret & Silzer, 1998, p. 3). Silzer and Jeanneret (2011) also wrote a classic article on the science and practice of individual executive assessment (see also Silzer et al., 2018).

CPs who wish to use executive assessments as a tool need to become well versed in the following foundational concepts in psychometrics:

- *Validity* is the extent to which an assessment instrument (a) measures what it purports to measure (*construct validity*) and, when used for selecting people for a position, (b) effectively predicts subsequent performance in the target position (*predictive validity*).

  Key reference sources for CPs who use assessments include the following: *The Standards for Educational and Psychological Testing* (6th ed.; American Educational Research Association, American Psychological Association, & National Council on Measurement in Education, 2014), *Principles for the Validation and Use of Personnel Selection Procedures* (Society for Industrial and Organizational Psychology, 2018), and the technical manual for the assessment being considered for use (which will be available from the test publisher).

- *Reliability* is the degree to which scores on an assessment are consistent and not subject to randomness, especially over time gaps.

  The following are examples of key leader effectiveness attributes and examples of standardized assessments that tap those characteristics that many CPs in APA Divisions 13 and 14 (Consulting Psychology and Industrial and Organizational Psychology, respectively) use to help identify leadership strengths and development needs (Vandaveer et al., 2019).

- *Cognitive ability* is analytical problem solving, general intellectual "horsepower," and logical thinking and analysis and includes inductive and deductive reasoning, visionary and strategic thinking, and emotional intelligence (EI) ability.

  Note that EI assessed as an ability can be especially helpful in developmental coaching when used in combination with 360-degree feedback, comparing one's EI ability with perceived effectiveness in interpersonal relationships and other "people-related skills." This allows for a more accurate identification of strategies for elevating the individual's effectiveness in key leadership skills and behaviors.

■ *Knowledge and skills* include functional knowledge and skills (e.g., finance, legal, information technology [IT], HR) and knowledge of the organization (e.g., its industry, history, business, position relative to competitors [if for profit], leadership principles, communication, organizational political navigation skills, to mention only a few).

Note that knowledge and cognitive skills tests are rarely used for executive development. Sometimes, for functional roles (e.g., accounting, IT, legal) or specialized roles, such tests will be used to select leaders, particularly external candidates. Internal candidates' knowledge and problem-solving skills are usually well known, having been demonstrated in their work. We rarely use cognitive ability and skills tests mainly because the client often does not want them used. Reasons vary, but among them are (a) not wanting to "insult" the candidate who, for example, has advanced university degrees and a strong record of success or other credible indicators (e.g., a trusted referral source who knows the individual well, public information such as publications) or (b) not seeing the relevance themselves of test items to the kind of problem solving done on the job (i.e., not fully understanding how assessed general intelligence ["horsepower"] relates to the kinds of complex business problems on the job that require a great deal of practical intelligence [usually] seasoned with significant experience).

There are situations in which cognitive ability testing makes practical sense, such as selecting employees for a nuclear power plant or other nuclear facility or other high-risk-of-catastrophe jobs. Cognitive ability and knowledge testing is also done for key jobs related to national security (e.g., U.S. Foreign Service, where our ambassadors come from; Federal Bureau of Investigation; Central Intelligence Agency).

■ *Personality* includes personal attributes that manifest in one's characteristic behavior, temperament, mannerisms, and so forth that originate from both "nature" (genes—inherited) and "nurture" (environment—learned behaviors).

Typically, these assessments are self-report inventories (question-naires) that assess key attributes important in leadership. Reputable assessments have been well validated and have norms against which to compare individuals' profiles. These assessments can be valuable in helping to understand key stakeholders' 360-degree feedback better because the profile often helps explain "why" for both positive feed-back and indicators of areas to improve.

Note that all self-report inventories of personality are fakeable—some more than others. That is, one can answer as they think they "should" rather than how they truly see themselves, leading to inaccu-rate assessment interpretations. Some assessments are more vulnerable to that than others. It is important that the CP has a solid understand-ing of psychometrics, reads and understands each assessment's technical manual, and keeps up-to-date with research on the instruments they use. There are several ways to determine the likelihood of excessive "faking," including some assessments' built-in validity ("fake") scales, "triangulating" by having two or more measures of key attributes, and a good assessment interview.

Typically, individuals taking these assessments for development purposes, knowing that the reports will be kept strictly confidential—they are only shared with their manager and whoever in TM may be responsible for shepherding their development—are motivated to respond as they truly see themselves versus responding to try to make the profile come out a certain way (which almost always trips them up such that they may not think the interpretation of the assessment is accurate).

We strongly advise that CPs and other types of leader coaches take formal courses in psychometric theory to ensure their understanding. Reading the test manual is not sufficient for adequately interpreting the assessment profiles. The assessor must be sufficiently versed in psycho-logical measurement that they well understand the strengths and the limitations of the particular assessment—that is, they are equipped to evaluate what is in the test manual. Taking a test publisher's certification course will be helpful but, in our view, not sufficient. Test publishers are motivated to sell their assessments; having enough knowledge to know what questions to ask and how to understand the answer in the course is important.

- *Motivational drivers and values* are related to leader effectiveness. Examples of drivers that these types of assessments measure are power, recognition, financial success, security, safety, altruism, adventure, intellectual challenge, and so forth.

A primary value of using psychological assessments in leader development coaching is the rich platform for dialogue between the client and CP that they provide, which often sparks new insights and learning. However, the caveat "properly used" includes the following:

- selecting the appropriate assessments for use—they are job related, have sound psychometric properties (e.g., they have internal consistency reliability, construct validity, which means the scales measure what they purport to measure, tested statistically), and provide findings likely to be useful for the client;
- ensuring the administration of the assessments is consistent with the guidelines from the technical report or testing manual (testing conditions must be the same as for the validation sample);
- understanding the measurement properties of each measure used (i.e., reliability, validity, interpretation of each construct)—the CP needs to have sufficient grounding in psychometrics to critically evaluate the tool and understand its strengths and limitations;
- having skill and experience in interpreting results and profiles for useful application with clients;
- ensuring the confidentiality of the assessment results, as agreed by all parties at the beginning of the coaching engagement (in the contracting phase), including the safekeeping of assessment results by a trained and qualified professional (often by a TM or other HR professional; more information about this can be found in Chapter 6);
- effectively using the assessment results to help identify clients' leadership strengths and suggest areas for development; and
- abiding by all legal and ethical considerations in using psychological assessments (see Chapter 6 for more on this subject).

Appropriate use of assessments means becoming thoroughly familiar with the instrument. Every high-quality published assessment has a technical manual that documents the assessment's development, psychometric properties, construct validation process and results, administration instructions, interpretive information, and usually, norms. Contact the test publisher for the manual, case studies of its use, appropriate norms, and certification training that may be offered. Keep in mind that the use of psychological tests (e.g., to evaluate ability, knowledge, personality, values, needs) impacts the lives and careers of individuals when key decisions will be made about the individual (selection, job placement, promotion, and development focus) and that the user of the assessments (i.e., the CP conducting the assessments) is fully responsible for ensuring the reliability, validity, and fairness of the assessments they use. The full extent of the CP's responsibility and potential liability in using assessments is described in Chapter 6.

In addition, the *Buros Mental Measurements Yearbook* is the comprehensive, authoritative resource exploring the entire field of published psychometrics. Go to https://marketplace.unl.edu/buros/ for information and an authoritative evaluation of the psychometric properties of an assessment instrument you are considering using. There are several extremely popular assessment instruments that have poor measurement properties and that Buros recommends against using. If Buros recommends against using an assessment, we strongly recommend following that advice.

As the CP begins using and experiencing good results with particular assessment instruments, they should be aware of an important caution from Marshall McLuhan, the famous Canadian philosopher, who said, "We shape our tools, and thereafter our tools shape us." Professionals, including coaches, tend to favor the tools with which they are familiar. Familiarity with favored tools can shape coaches' thinking about the topic being measured, such as management or leadership. That is, it is easy to begin thinking about the characteristics of an effective leader in terms of the assessments one uses—rather than effectively evaluating the role, context, and culture of the coaching client's position or desired position and then selecting assessment instruments that assess the critical factors for that particular role. CPs must remain constantly aware that assessments are fallible and need to be chosen according to what is likely to be useful in coaching a specific leader. Some consulting firms and client organizations have favored certain assessments or even assessment batteries, so CPs employed by them do not always have a choice in what assessments will be used. However, CPs always have a choice about how much emphasis to place on interpreted results. The guiding principle should be the appropriateness for the particular position and company and their usefulness to the client.

Review of Past Performance Appraisals and Other Information About the Client

Organizations regularly review individuals' performance for use in employee development and often also to help determine pay treatment each year. In most cases, coaching clients may have had multiple performance appraisals, development plans, TM reviews, or 360-degree feedback processes tied to formal performance evaluation. The CP and client together should decide on the relevance of existing materials for the client's development. Even if this material is offered to the coach by HR sponsors of coaching, it is best if the coach and client make the decision together about its usefulness as early input to coaching.

Observing Coaching Clients During Coaching Meetings and in the Workplace

Direct observation of the client at work, also called *shadowing a client* (Frisch et al., 2012), can be useful in obtaining additional information about the client as leader. Examples include observing the client making a board presentation, conducting a town hall–style meeting for all employees and leading their management team meetings. Coach–client dialogue about these opportunities for real-time observation can be useful in helping form hypotheses about why certain situations are challenging and what may help improve effectiveness in those situations. As with any hypothesis about client behavior and its influences, the coach should remain open to multiple interpretations and avoid confirmation bias in which expectations shape perceptions. Coaches need to build the ability to understand the client's behavior from multiple perspectives and thereby expand clients' self-insight.

Often, client presentations are recorded for asynchronous listening by stakeholders in the organization. Where public speaking or impact is a development need, no feedback is more powerful than seeing and hearing oneself in action. Using an actual speech from the client's leadership responsibilities or using practice recordings during coaching meetings can be invaluable in helping the client analyze what was particularly effective and why and what could be improved in both message and delivery. This real-time feedback with clients is much more impactful than only debriefing from the client's memory of a presentation.

Development Plans

Many coaching engagements include preparation of a professional development plan as an important element in the success of the developmental process (Frisch et al., 2012; Hernez-Broome & Boyce, 2011). In shorter coaching engagements, such as those in Level 1 coaching, a draft development plan may be the main outcome of the effort. In typical Level 3 coaching, development plans may evolve as the engagement progresses. A working development plan may be shaped by the coach and client after just a few meetings. It then may evolve, with clearer goals and more direct-action ideas after stakeholder feedback or other assessments. By the midpoint of such an engagement, a shareable development plan is often discussed with sponsors, resulting in a version that all can support (see Figure 2.1 for the typical sequence of these steps).

A working development plan, especially early in an engagement, facilitates active dialogue and brainstorming between the CP and client about (a) what "more effective" will look like, (b) critical success factors for achieving the goals, and (c) behaviors to implement and experiments to try between coaching meetings. As the plan is tested, refined, and vetted with sponsors, more specificity can describe what developmental success will look like and how it might be observed and measured.

Various formats for development plans exist (see Frisch et al., 2012). However, an element that is often overlooked is the client's strengths. There is a tendency for clients, sponsors, and even coaches to focus on the gap areas or deficiencies. Positive psychology encourages building on strengths, and certainly, having a coach and client dig into a deeper understanding of the client's strengths is a valuable part of coaching. We encourage that strengths be included in development plans. Clients often need help in how to structure a development plan (note that some organizations have a preferred structure), but once the structure is set and coach and client brainstorm and evolve content, it is best if the client is the prime mover in drafting and owning the development plan.

TECHNIQUES

Communication: Listening, Dialogue, Question Frameworks

CPs employ a variety of techniques to facilitate learning—in the coaching meeting and between meetings. The following are a few examples.

Listening

Listening is one of the most important skills the CP must have and keep honing. Really listening—to hear and understand what the other person means—requires focused attention (to the client's words, affect, and accompanying behaviors). It is important to restate what you are hearing to ensure that you correctly heard what the client is actually intending to say. We call this *clear listening*—that is, listening from the client's perspective.

Dialogue

In the coaching meeting—and the occasional between-meeting conversation—the primary method of conversation is dialogue. *Dialogue*, which is different from discussion, is defined as "a conversation in which people think together in relationship" (Isaacs, 1999). Isaacs defined dialogue as

- "a reflective learning process" (pp. 38, 272);
- a "shared inquiry, a way of thinking and reflecting together" (p. 9);

- involving "giving up the effort to make them (the other person) understand us and come to a greater understanding of ourselves and each other" (p. 9);
- "relaxing our grip on certainty and listening to the possibilities that result simply from being in relationship with others" (p. 19);
- "harnessing the collective intelligence" (p. 11); and
- "the most important parts . . . that neither party could have imagined when starting" (p. 9).

Isaacs (1999) emphasized that discussion is for making a decision. Thus, discussion is used, for example, when creating the development plan. When working to come to a decision, the client and coach converse to come to closure on what the plan will be and how it will be articulated in the written development plan document.

Question Frameworks

In the coaching meeting, various question frameworks are used to facilitate the client's learning. A *question framework* is an organized structure of questions tailored to the purpose of a given stage in the coaching model employed (Stoltzfus, 2008; Stout-Rostron, 2014). The following is an example of a four-stage question framework using the GROW model (see page 23) in Level 1 coaching engagements (behavioral approach).

For G (goal), the CP might ask: "What do you want to accomplish in our work together? What is your goal?" (This gets at the coaching goal and also the goal for this meeting.) "At the end of our coaching engagement, what do you most want to have achieved? How will we know we've achieved it?" "What would you like to accomplish in today's session?"

For R (reality), the CP might ask: "What have you done so far toward your goal?" "What do you think may have inhibited achievement of your goal when you have worked toward it in the past?" "Describe for me your thought process: how you decided what to try (cognitive behavioral approach), what you did, what the result was, and what you did in response to that result." "As you reflect on your efforts and the outcome, what may have caused less progress than you had hoped? What assumptions underlie your approach?"

For O (options), the CP might ask: "What do you see as your options right now?" "Let's brainstorm all the different things you might do to achieve what you want." "What will be required to do each thing?"

For W (what will you do?), the CP might ask: "What will you do differently from before? When will you do it?" "What support do you need?"

In Level 3 leader and executive coaching and when using a cognitive behavioral approach, the CP focuses the client on thoughts and feelings as well as behaviors. Still using the GROW model, in the R phase, the client may have generated one or more ideas about why what they have tried didn't work—or didn't work well enough—or perhaps why they haven't tried certain things to achieve their goal. The CP may recognize or suspect some unfounded or self-limiting assumptions the client is making, a misinterpretation of others' behaviors, and so on. The CP might say, "Describe for me what you were thinking that led to the decision to try X," and "What did you experience in trying that approach? Include both what you thought and what you felt and how you interpreted others' reactions." Then follow that thread, listening carefully and supportively to the client's relaying their thought and decision process, what they experienced, how they interpreted the outcome, and to what they attributed the failure to achieve the desired result. Engage the client in dialogue (see the definition on page 98) and joint meaning making as you analyze together what happened. The CP must listen deeply to the client's words, observe their affect when "reliving" the experience, and describe to what they attribute the approach not having worked. Listening from the client's perspective and engaging in dialogue ("thinking together") often leads to insight that is useful in planning a different approach to achieve the goal.

If the client expresses doubt or negative feelings, the CP will facilitate the client in examining where those negative and likely self-defeating feelings are coming from, and they may engage in cognitive reframing (another technique, described next).

In the Options phase, the CP helps the client brainstorm options openly, facilitating the client's examination of their assumptions, shining a bright light on them and dispelling those that are unnecessarily sabotaging efforts to achieve the goal. One question might be, "What are you thinking and feeling as you contemplate what you will do?"

For descriptions of other question frameworks and many illustrative examples, see Stout-Rostron's (2014) book, *Business Coaching International: Transforming Individuals and Organizations* (2nd ed.).

Cognitive Reframing

Cognitive reframing is the process of identifying and examining how the client experiences situations or events and how the client is thinking about things. If their thinking is irrational or otherwise unfounded (e.g., negative thinking, pessimism, catastrophizing, or other kinds of self-defeating thoughts and beliefs), the client is challenged and helped to change the way they are thinking, changing their mindset. For more information on this useful technique, see Ducharme (2004).

Stout-Rostron (2014) said the following about question frameworks and cognitive reframing: "What is shown to be transformative and to create the greatest change in the coaching conversation is the identification and transformation of limiting assumptions into empowering assumptions through the use of a question process" (p. 112).

Role-Playing

Role-playing can be an effective tool for practicing new behaviors and different ways of thinking. For example, if a client wants to be more effective in resolving conflict with a peer, the CP may assume the role of that colleague, and the client and CP act out a scenario that replicates what happens between the client and their peer. Then the client and CP analyze the interaction together: "When you said X, and she said Y, what were you feeling? What were you thinking? Then when you said Z in response to what she said, what happened? Why might she have reacted the way she did?" The CP facilitates the client in analyzing the interaction, identifying likely causes for the conflict that arose and what alternative approaches the client could take that might be more effective. Note that these are prime examples of the CP's use of their dialogic self.

Cognitive and Affective Perspective Taking

Cognitive and affective perspective taking are important techniques for helping the client strengthen their ability to (a) infer the other person's thoughts or beliefs (cognition) and (b) infer another person's feelings or emotions (affect). Cognitive perspective taking involves changing one's mental set (perspective), while affective perspective taking draws more on one's degree of emotional intelligence (Healey & Grossman, 2018).

Client Storytelling and CP Use of Metaphor

Drawing from attachment theory in developmental psychology and current neuroscience research, this technique helps the coaching client and the coach understand the client's narrative about themselves, which comes from the cognitive and relational patterns they developed as children. Drawing out the client's story about themselves is rich, fertile ground for introspection, reflection, and change (Drake, 2009).

The premise underlying this technique is that "the stories clients tell in coaching are often windows into the larger narrative patterns in their life" (Drake, 2009, p. 53). Examining those together and identifying thought patterns that may be self-limiting at best—or, at worst, self-defeating— can allow the work of coaching to help the client rewrite their script on themselves and get unstuck from thought and behavior patterns that stand in the way of achieving leadership excellence.

We encourage CPs to draw from their life experiences to create metaphors that hopefully resonate with a client to foster insight. Reflecting on our key life experiences, observations of nature, skills we struggle to develop, recovering from setbacks, and so forth can be sources of ideas that fuel the CP's metaphoric thinking that may be useful for sparking insights in clients. This is not about the coach telling life stories, which is inappropriate. This is about the coach extracting key life lessons, often in metaphorical images, to trigger a new perspective or help a client see things differently. This assumes CPs regularly use their human capacity for meaning making (the dialogic self) to extract images and learnings that can be useful with clients.

Homework

Between coaching meetings, a lot of important work gets done. Homework assignments may include relevant articles to read (e.g., on leadership, organizational power dynamics, executive presence, other things specific to the client's development work), new behaviors to try, feedback to request from other colleagues, self-reflection exercises in the form of thought-provoking questions to ask oneself, writing reflections, journaling their story, and any of a variety of other learning-enhancing activities. Ideally, homework is both conceptually and practically tied to whatever version of a development plan is driving the coaching forward.

Some CPs encourage client journaling between meetings as the process proceeds. Extending the insights that emerge through interviewing the client, brainstorming actions, and debriefing behavioral experiments, journaling encourages the practice of self-reflection. In the study by Vandaveer et al. (2016), 15% of participants said they asked clients to use journaling in most of their engagements. Not all clients will take to this practice naturally, but most will understand the point of continuing to reflect between coaching meetings. Certainly, an implicit objective of coaching, consistent with the time-limited aspect of coaching, is fostering curiosity in clients about why they do what they do, how they feel about interactions with others, and what they might do differently. Journaling can be a key aspect of helping clients learn how they learn and how to continue learning, a process that has been labeled the *double-loop* of learning (Argyris & Schön, 1974). Client insights about preferred methods of learning, whatever those are for each individual, are as valuable as the learning itself. Journaling is a tangible means to encourage that double-loop learning.

Follow-Up

As a frequent part of the closure of coaching, CPs typically build in one or two postcoaching touchpoints by phone or online to follow up. It is best if the expectations for this are set up as an extrapolation of the engagement (in the contracting phase) rather than seeking to set these up later. Clients appreciate that they can reach out to the coach with questions or for just-in-time support on a challenge, but coaches should not feel the same freedom. Follow-up with the client should be arranged in advance.

The exception is when the CP becomes aware that the client has been promoted, changed jobs, or left the organization. To the extent that CPs are aware of such changes, possibly through other contacts in the organization or social media announcements, a congratulatory collegial email is certainly warranted that demonstrates caring without any expectation of renewing coaching. It is gratifying when past clients in new jobs or organizations reach out to reengage in coaching, but these opportunities need to be driven by the client.

If the coaching engagement was initiated by HR or TM, CPs can feel free to follow up with HR sponsors. CPs who are proactive in asking for whatever feedback can be shared are more likely to obtain it; also, building ongoing professional relationships with them is encouraged because they are often sources of the coach's future work.

If the coaching engagement was initiated directly with line management (typically the client's manager), occasional follow-up calls to the manager to see how things are going are appropriate—if specified in the contracting phase of coaching that the CP will be doing that.

This is quite a lot to think about, but coaching is a forgiving process; new tools can be tried at the next session, and there are many roads to helping the client. CPs are encouraged to engage in self-reflection as they prepare for—and conclude—each session, always mindful of their role in facilitating the client's learning and fully supporting the client. The list of tools, methods, and techniques provided earlier in the chapter can help coaches both plan and debrief coaching meetings so that coach and client are in a parallel growth trajectory, although in quite different domains.

SUMMARY

This chapter covered a lot of territory about the inner workings of the coaching process, including descriptions of the primary tools (the CP's self, the CP–client relationship, theoretical frameworks, and coaching models); methods, such as coaching meetings and the coaching conversation, goal setting, and measuring progress; and some of the primary techniques used by CPs to help facilitate the client's learning.

We turn next to the important question: How effective is executive coaching?

4

How Effective Is Executive Coaching?

A typical organization's investment in individual coaching for its leaders is significant. Forbes estimated that companies in the United States spend $366 billion annually on leadership development (Westfall, 2019). According to a 2019 survey of 28,000 business leaders conducted by *Chief Learning Officer* magazine, 74% of organizations use instructor-led leadership training and 63% use executive coaching (Prokopeak, 2018). The Conference Board's Global Executive Coaching Survey 2018 (with 190 respondents) showed that average annual spending on external executive coaching ranges from $200,000 to over $1 million, with about half spending less than $500,000. The popularity and use of executive coaching for enhancing leader effectiveness and preparing leaders for advancement to higher organizational levels continue to grow every year, so clearly, organizations are finding value. This chapter summarizes the state of the

https://doi.org/10.1037/0000293-005
Coaching Psychology: Catalyzing Excellence in Organizational Leadership, by V. V. Vandaveer and M. H. Frisch

science at this writing regarding the effectiveness of coaching leaders in organizations.

Measuring coaching effectiveness has remained difficult for a variety of reasons, primarily methodological challenges (Athanasopoulou & Dopson, 2018; De Meuse et al., 2009; Graßmann et al., 2020; Grover & Furnham, 2016; Hernez-Broome & Boyce, 2011; Jones et al., 2016; Osatuke et al., 2017; Williams & Lowman, 2018). The research to date is organized here as follows:

- the **"criterion problem"** (i.e., the dependent variable), including self-assessment, perceptions of others, demonstration of leadership competencies, affective outcome (e.g., job satisfaction), and organization performance, typically measured as return on investment (ROI) in coaching;
- **moderator variables** (i.e., independent variables), factors that moderate coaching effectiveness, such as attributes of the coach and coachee, the coach's status (internal or external to the organization), and the nature and quality of the coach–client relationship;
- **methodological problems**—meta-analyses or single study; and
- **discussion**—implications for coaching psychologists (CPs).

THE "CRITERION PROBLEM" (DEPENDENT VARIABLE)

For many different reasons, it is difficult to isolate the impact of coaching on leader effectiveness, not the least of which is that many other factors affect a leader's and the organization's performance. Nevertheless, there are increasing numbers of studies attempting to elucidate the impact of coaching on outcomes of interest. The majority of studies are retrospective and use short-term affective reactions or perceptions of effectiveness as outcomes. Some studies have attempted to measure ROI in coaching. And increasingly, there are meta-analyses of coaching studies.

Methods of measuring the effectiveness of coaching have typically included the coach's self-assessment, perceptions of the coachee's key stakeholders (i.e., multisource or 360-degree feedback), assessment of changes in skill or behaviors, and changes in attributes of the coachee (e.g., sense of self-efficacy).

Self-Assessment

The coachee's self-assessment often involves ratings relative to goal attainment, satisfaction with the coaching process and outcomes, and self-efficacy. The coachee's satisfaction with coaching has been shown to be highly related to the perceived quality of the working alliance between coach and CP (Baron & Morin, 2010; Graßmann et al., 2020; Jones et al., 2016).

Perceptions of Others

Gathering key stakeholders' feedback through 360-degree feedback, when well done, can be useful for informing the coaching work and clarifying specific goals. Of course, as with anything else, the quality and usefulness of the output are to a large extent determined by the quality of the input, which requires, among other things, a well-designed feedback process and instrument. In one study that specifically looked at the relationship of multisource feedback on coaching outcomes, the researchers concluded that "the effect was greater on outcomes when coaching was provided without multisource feedback" (Jones et al., 2016, p. 16). However, there are some methodological issues that call that conclusion into question. As an example, using "multisource feedback" as a binary independent variable (e.g., used or not used in coaching) is problematic in several ways, including differences across coaching cases in method, format, nature of questions asked; differences in the method of administration; differences in the nature and quality of feedback of the multisource feedback results; and differences in culture (country and organizational) across organizational settings (e.g., a culture in which feedback is routine, welcomed, and used effectively vs. not). In addition, the noncomparability of multisource methods and/or instruments, administration, and characteristics of the feedback, in our view, render these results not useful.

For example, if 360-degree feedback is obtained through questionnaire survey, differences across organizations in survey content and method of administration and the nature and quality of feedback provided (e.g., across coaches, countries and cultures, type, size of organization) would certainly depress correlations with criteria of interest (which are also different across studies). If 360-degree feedback is obtained by interview, comparisons across companies, situations, type of interview conducted, expertise of the interviewee, and so forth are also difficult and statistical correlations naturally not high.

Another source of the potential skewing of the results is 360-degree feedback participants choosing the feedback participants without vetting by the client's manager. That is, sometimes coaches select participants who they know will give them positive feedback instead of selecting participants who represent the range of perspectives to get the truest picture possible.

Nowack and Mashihi (2012) examined the strengths and limitations of using 360-degree feedback to assess the effectiveness of coaching and identify typical reactions to feedback from different kinds of clients and implications for feedback and development strategies. Their findings indicated that although the purposes of 360-degree feedback are to (a) increase the client's awareness of how they and their performance are perceived by key others and (b) facilitate behavior change, the impact of such feedback can sometimes negatively affect the individual and their subsequent performance. Key factors contributing to the derailment of 360-degree feedback achieving its purposes included, among some other factors, such things as the ratio of positive to negative feedback if less than 3:1, how the feedback is delivered, the client's emotional response to the feedback, personality of the client, the client's receptiveness to feedback and readiness to change, and the coach's skill in helping the client understand, accept, value, and be motivated to use the feedback to help improve their effectiveness.

In Chapter 3, the tool of key stakeholder 360-degree feedback was described as one way to assess the perceptions of key stakeholders about the client's effectiveness. Assuming a well-designed and well-administered

360-degree feedback process, if conducted early in the coaching engagement to help identify perceived standout leadership strengths and focus areas for development, a brief, Time 2 360-degree feedback can be conducted toward the end of the coaching engagement. The Time 2 feedback can be conducted in person or electronically with a representative sample (or all) of the key stakeholders who participated in Time 1 feedback, or it can take the form of a brief follow-up survey that focuses on observed changes (Peterson, 1993). However, as Nowack and Mashihi (2012) found, the impact and effectiveness of 360-degree feedback depend on many factors, and the coach must be keenly aware of the factors that typically contribute to the desired positive impact and those that probably do not. CPs must recognize the possibility of derailment and backfiring if 360-degree feedback is not well constructed, -conducted, and -interpreted.

Another invaluable form of feedback is that obtained from professional peers in peer consultations, described in Chapter 3. Reviewing cases (anonymously with respect to the name of company, individual, and others) with other psychologists (preferably from different areas of psychology when possible) is tremendously helpful to the CP's continuing development toward professional expertise mastery. In addition, borrowing from a long tradition of counseling and clinical helpers, it is helpful to the CP's learning to build reflective activities into their work, such as case notes, journaling, and writing up each case for review in peer consults. These are essential aspects of foundational professional education and ongoing training of those in helping professions (Clay, 2017), and they apply directly to coaching.

Cognitive, Skill-Based, and Affective Criteria

The meta-analysis conducted by Jones et al. (2016) examined cognitive, skill-based, and affective outcome criteria and concluded that coaching had positive outcomes on organizational outcomes overall and on skill-based (i.e., competencies) and affective criteria (i.e., enhanced self-efficacy and confidence, increased job satisfaction and motivation, and stress reduction). Cognitive outcomes (i.e., declarative knowledge, procedural knowledge, and problem-solving strategies) were measured by recognition and recall tests. Skill-based outcomes (i.e., compilation and automaticity of new skills—e.g., leadership skills, technical skills) were measured by behavioral observation as reported in a multisource feedback questionnaire (the limitations of which were discussed previously). These researchers found that the effects of coaching on outcomes were stronger for internal than external coaches. Not knowing more about the coaches (e.g., levels and types of expertise), the results and conclusions from this study cannot be generalized across organizations and situations. However, the results do point to the need for a more in-depth look at internal and external coaches and the key attributes of each that relate to greater effectiveness.

Organizational Performance (ROI)

Some researchers have attempted to measure the ROI of coaching, described most clearly by De Meuse et al. (2009):

> The ROI metric depends on two key factors: (a) the overall cost an organization incurs implementing the coaching engagement, and (b) the financial benefits it obtains. These items are extremely difficult to measure and are highly unique to the specific coaching assignment. Obviously, the fee structure of different coaches varies greatly. Likewise, the organizational level and size of company of the coachee varies greatly. A Chief Executive Officer (CEO) can have a powerful impact on an organization. Some executives work on million-dollar deals, while others work on billion-dollar ones. In order to make meaningful conclusions regarding ROI, and to compare ROI across studies, all facets of the coaching engagement must be considered and measured, including the coaching costs and executives' enhanced organizational value. Such factors as the expertise of the coach, length of coaching engagement, and organizational support for the coaching also may play a pivotal role in success. In addition, the level of motivation and commitment of the executive who is being coached must be considered. We are not stating that it is impossible

to compute ROI, but it certainly is very, very difficult to do so. (pp. 125–126)

Controversy remains about estimating the dollar value of management and leadership behavior. Another factor that makes these studies controversial is the multidetermined and distal aspect of any organizational outcome, including both uncontrolled factors in the organization itself and the wider industry or context of the organization, as well as the time lag after coaching that would be required to have any management or leadership changes influence outcomes. Are 3 months enough? Is a year too long? Any rigorous study of Level 3 ROI coaching outcomes must acknowledge these uncontrolled variables in reaching conclusions about coaching effectiveness (De Meuse et al., 2009; O'Neil, 2000).

MODERATOR (INDEPENDENT) VARIABLES

Coach and Client Characteristics

Kilburg (2000) identified factors related to less successful outcomes with respect to the client and coach. Attributes of the client related to less successful outcomes were lack of motivation, unrealistic expectations of the coach or the coaching process, lack of follow-through on homework or intervention suggestions, severe psychopathology, and severe interpersonal problems. Attributes of the coach related to less successful outcomes included insufficient empathy with the client, lack of interest or expertise in the client's problem or issues, underestimating the severity of the client's problems or overestimating the coach's ability to influence the client, and significant or protracted negative countertransference (i.e., the coach overreacts to the client emotionally or has echoes of past significant, problematic relationships not managed appropriately; poor technique; or major or prolonged disagreements with the client about the coaching process).

In addition, attributes of the CP—in particular, communication skill, commitment, and capacity to generate trust—have been shown to influence the client's learning directly, even when the client's coaching experience is not particularly satisfying (Albizu et al., 2019).

Coach–Client Working Alliance

De Haan et al.'s (2013, 2016) studies showed that the coach's ability to build an effective working alliance yielded stronger ties with coaching effectiveness than the coach–client relationship variables alone.

De Haan and colleagues (2013, 2016, 2019, 2020; McKenna & Davis, 2009), using two large-scale randomized controlled studies—one longitudinal, took a deeper look at the impact of the quality of the working alliance between client and coach, prior research having indicated that as the major factor in coaching outcomes. Their studies showed that the client's resilience scores were good predictors of coaching outcomes, and in fact, they mediated the relationships between the felt quality of the working relationship and outcomes:

> The coachee will rate all aspects of the coaching experience as better or worse, in accordance with how useful the general experience was for them and their own optimism about these kinds of experiences (significantly influenced by coachee-based factors such as hope, expectancy, self-efficacy, resilience, mental well-being, and now, in our view, working alliance). (de Haan et al., 2020, p. 164)

Coach Status (Internal or External)

Moen and Skaalvik (2009), in a year-long study of 144 executives and middle managers in a Fortune 500 high-tech company, found significant positive effects of external coaching on the client's self-efficacy, goal setting, intrapersonal causal attributions of success, and need satisfaction. Significant positive effects of coaching by internal trained leaders of middle managers were also found for self-efficacy (only); however, the effects were not as strong as those from coaching by external professional coaches. While these findings and conclusions are interesting (and opposite to those of Jones et al., 2016), it is still the case that more needs to be known about the coaches and their attributes (e.g., knowledge, expertise, type of training or preparation for coaching) besides being external or internal.

METHODOLOGICAL PROBLEMS

Sample Bias

Low participation rate and/or criterion samples consisting of a limited select number of raters—for example, the client's and their supervisor's ratings—may not reflect the larger key stakeholder pool's perceptions (Williams & Lowman, 2018).

Inadequate Numbers of Studies

In addition, as De Meuse et al. (2009) reported, "the **inadequate numbers of studies** in the meta-analysis (of the available empirical studies) and the failure of authors to report sufficient information about the coaching intervention itself preclude us from identifying when coaching will or will not lead to positive results" (p. 121).

Noncomparability of Studies

"The coaching outcomes research is characterized by high heterogeneity of issues, problems and goals. This makes the comparison across studies difficult" (Athanasopoulou & Dopson, 2018, p. 73).

Flawed Methodologies

As Osatuke and colleagues (2017) pointed out, using the scientific method to study the humanistic change facilitation processes of coaching that "reflect how people grapple with meanings" (p. 173) is flawed:

> Accurately capturing meaning-making processes that take place in a coaching context . . . requires tools of study that afford for a substantial fluidity and subjectivity of the evaluated interpersonally based development. These tools should account for scenarios where priorities may change throughout coaching. (p. 173)

The use of classic measurement evaluation approaches, often rooted in the scientific method,

> misses the mark due to misalignment between the humanistic process
> of intervention and scientific method of evaluation. . . . In addition,
> very few studies focus on organizational-level outcomes. EC [execu-
> tive coaching] outcome research erroneously treats coaching as an
> individual-level intervention rather than a social process with active
> involvement of multiple stakeholders. (Osatuke et al., 2017, p. 173)

That is, there is a fundamental mismatch between the nature and process of coaching and the classic standardized scientific evaluation methods typically used to study the effectiveness of coaching.

Despite the significant difficulties in assessing coaching outcomes, researchers have nevertheless made some headway in understanding some of the factors related to coaching effectiveness, however it was measured. In his meta-analysis of six empirical studies examining executive skill and job performance improvement, De Meuse et al. (2009) concluded that (a) executive coaching "generally leads to a moderate-to-large improve-ment in coachees' skill and performance ratings" (p. 129); (b) coachees' self-ratings of improvement were higher than others' ratings, but both were considered to be a moderate-to-large amount of improvement; and (c) coaching results in inconsistent monetary returns.

DISCUSSION: IMPLICATIONS FOR CPs

CPs, in initial meetings with a prospective coaching client, need to be prepared to answer the question "How can you tell if your coaching is effective?" One's answer can include the several different ways they have assessed coaching outcomes, as well as other possible ways, followed by asking the prospective client if they have preferred ways of assessing outcomes. Some organizations have a standard process for evaluating coaching outcomes; others look to the CP for recommending the best approach.

The outcomes of the CP's work with a client typically take a while to become measurable. In the interim, CPs are encouraged to periodically seek feedback from the client and the client's manager (with the client's agreement, of course), and then the more formal feedback will be received after the end of the coaching engagement.

Other opportunities for feedback to the CP—in addition to 360-degree feedback—that are built into the arc of the coaching engagement include (a) reviewing the client's draft development plan with the manager and sponsors, if applicable; and (b) conducting, in the final phase of the coaching engagement, a bookend meeting that reviews the engagement, progress achieved, and plans for the client's ongoing learning and development as a leader. Opportunities for the CP to request and receive feedback at those points are natural and useful for the CP and the client's learning. Should any of the feedback to the CP contain mixed or concerning messages, the CP has the opportunity to make adjustments that will benefit the client's (and CP's) outcomes.

With respect to the more formal evaluation that occurs after coaching has concluded, the general methods in applied program evaluation research that are applicable to coaching include the following criterion measures:

- the client's key learnings;
- what the client did to apply those learnings and what the outcomes were;
- what impact the client's actions in applying learnings had on their performance and leadership effectiveness and the wider organization (e.g., business results and other desired outcomes);
- observed on-the-job behavior change (by the client, the manager, and other key stakeholders);
- the degree to which the client and manager attribute to coaching the assessed impact on outcomes of importance;
- level of satisfaction with the experience; and
- the degree of confidence that the client and manager have, respectively, in their estimates of impact and value (Anderson, 2011; Ely & Zaccaro, 2011; Kirkpatrick, 1976, 1994; Steinbrenner & Schlosser, 2011).

CPs are encouraged to identify effective methods of assessing the effectiveness of coaching and share their learnings by publishing the results or presenting their studies at professional conferences.

SUMMARY

This chapter presented the research to date on the effectiveness of organizational leader coaching. The primary research methods, the strengths and limitations of each, and the findings and conclusions drawn thus far were reviewed. We hope that the reader—and researchers who are studying coaching effectiveness—will pay special attention to the Osatuke et al. (2017) study regarding flawed methodologies and their overall conclusions. That is, the use of nomothetic methods (i.e., generalizing results from large-sample statistical analyses of selected variables) is inappropriate for studying the idiographic one-on-one helping process.[1]

---

[1] *Idiographic assessment* emphasizes the subjective, unique experiences of the individual, and the coach and coachee together interpret meaning over time. *Nomothetic assessment* is the analysis of quantitative data from a large number of people and its generalization to the population, using statistical norms to predict individuals' behavior or performance.

5

How Psychologists Can Prepare for Coaching Leaders

This chapter highlights several major points about preparing for leadership coaching. We explore the importance of understanding aspects of the "job" or role of a leader in an organization, the nature of the context in which a leader must be effective (which requires an in-depth understanding of organizations in general), and the knowledge, skills, and personal characteristics needed for leadership roles in general. Although going back to school and getting a general business degree is not necessary, the more the coaching psychologist (CP) understands about the world of organizational leaders—and what is required to be a truly great leader who inspires the best performance from others (Boyatzis & McKee, 2005)— the more effective they will be in helping leaders grow and achieve their leadership potential.

We then turn our attention to what the job of leader coaching entails, citing research on what foundational knowledge, skills, and personal

https://doi.org/10.1037/0000293-006
Coaching Psychology: Catalyzing Excellence in Organizational Leadership, by V. V. Vandaveer and M. H. Frisch

attributes are important for being an effective CP and what additional knowledge and competencies are needed beyond one's graduate training in psychology, with suggestions for acquiring them and building. As noted in the article by Vandaveer et al. (2016), executive and leader coaching was pioneered by psychologist practitioners, and for many years, coaching was supported scientifically by the theories and frameworks of the CP's area of graduate training—for example, industrial and organizational (I/O) psychologists coached from the rich evidence bases in organizational dynamics, leadership, motivation, social psychology, psychometrics (individual assessment), and group dynamics (Vandaveer, 2020); clinical psychologists from clinical, psychodynamic, cognitive behavioral, humanistic, and systems and family systems dynamics; and cognitive psychologists from cognitive, developmental, and neuroscience. Only more recently has a strong science base supporting coaching psychology as a professional practice area of psychology been developing (Bachkirova, 2016; de Haan et al., 2013, 2016, 2020; De Meuse et al., 2009; Grant, 2013; Grant & Cavanagh, 2007; Grant et al., 2010; Lane & Corrie, 2009; Laske, 2007; Palmer & Whybrow, 2008; Passmore, 2007; Steinbrenner & Schlosser, 2011; Vandaveer et al., 2016; Wasylyshyn, 2003, 2017; Williams & Lowman, 2018). One conclusion from the foundational competency study (Vandaveer et al., 2016) was that no one emerging from any doctoral or master's program in psychology was sufficiently prepared to do executive coaching; more knowledge and skills from other domains of psychology are needed, as well as supervised practice.

ATTRIBUTES OF EFFECTIVE LEADERSHIP COACHES

From the perspective of more than 25 years of doing executive coaching and being mentored and coached by highly effective executive coaching psychologists, I (VV) identified 13 attributes of highly effective coaches (all of which happen to begin with the letter C): confidentiality, competence, candor, caring, courage, commitment, conscientiousness, curiosity and agile learning, calmness and centeredness, cultural competence, compassion, consistency, and continuous learning (Vandaveer, 2012b). This list is from personal reflections, experience, and observations of and interactions with successful CPs.

At this point in the United States, it is the responsibility of the aspiring coach to learn and build the important coaching psychology competencies because currently, there are no uniform guidelines or standards for the practice of coaching psychology. Building the critical knowledge and skills can be done through graduate coursework and internships, postgraduate on-the-job learning and development (e.g., as part of a consultancy that does executive coaching), professional society workshops that offer American Psychological Association (APA)–approved continuing education (CE) credits, peer consultation and peer "supervision," and shadowing a CP as they work with a client. The latter method is difficult to do because coaching work is private and confidential, and the client could feel uncomfortable having an observer in the meeting with their CP. However, occasionally (especially in Level 1 coaching, which are limited engagements at the behavioral level of work), such shadowing may be possible.

THEORETICAL FOUNDATIONS AND COMPETENCY FRAMEWORKS

The science of human behavior, including in organizations and leadership, and much of the foundational knowledge and skills identified in the study by Vandaveer et al. (2016), are part of the core of graduate training in psychology in the United States. However, training in one graduate program is not sufficient for doing executive coaching; everyone needs knowledge and skills from other psychology areas.

Clinical and counseling psychologists, for example, typically need to add knowledge of organizational psychology, business principles, social psychology, general systems theory, principles of adult learning, principles of leadership-team effectiveness, and working with the person in the organizational context, as well as a good grounding in psychometrics. Although many have experience working with family systems, that approach differs significantly from business organizational systems. Not knowing what they don't know, a good number of health service psychologists working in organizations often end up practicing "therapy" but with the label of *coaching*, as mentioned in Chapter 1.

Similarly, I/O psychologists need grounding in the theories and practice domains of working in a one-on-one helping relationship. As discussed in Chapter 3, this is not an easy transition, particularly for those steeped in statistical analysis and prediction of leader effectiveness. Changing to working with leaders to help them develop as leaders—and to (it is hoped) defy I/O psychologists' predictions of how effective they will be as leaders—is a very different skill set. However, the knowledge from I/O training and practice is invaluable for rigorous thinking; awareness of assumptions and measurement error (e.g., our impressions and analysis or assessment of what the individual says); individual differences; perception; the social psychology and power dynamics of organizations; job and role analysis and required knowledge, skills, abilities, and personal characteristics; psychometrics; and many other things.

No matter which area of graduate training in psychology one comes from, the CP will have a wealth of knowledge and skills that will always be useful in leader coaching, but they also need to work to add to their repertoire of knowledge, skills, understanding, and perspective (Lee & Frisch, 2011, 2015; Vandaveer et al., 2016).

Table 5.1 (which is Table 15 from the study by Vandaveer et al., 2016, p. 139) shows a summary of the foundational competencies identified by 27 subject matter experts (SMEs), who were recognized as among the top executive CPs in the United States, and by the sample of 342 I/O and consulting psychologists who responded to the Practice Analysis Survey that was developed from the SMEs' data. Referring to this table, psychologists can identify the theoretical frameworks and knowledge and skill areas to add to their repertoire, as well as important personal characteristics to hone and types of experiences to acquire. Although it is not necessary for a psychologist to go back to graduate school for another degree, everyone will need to figure out how best to acquire additional important competencies.

Table 5.1

Foundational Coaching Psychology Competency Model: Overview

Coaching context

1. Organizational characteristics and culture	2. Coachee characteristics, role, readiness
3. Coach characteristics, expertise, experience	4. Coaching purposes, goals
	5. Duration and stage of coaching

Foundational coaching psychology competencies (KSAPs)

Coaching psychology process	Knowledge	Skills	Personal characteristics
1. **Initial needs assessment and client qualification**	**Theory/discipline**	**Cognitive, analytical/technical**	■ Integrity/honesty
2. **Contracting**—agreement regarding expectations, roles, processes, rules, fees	■ Consulting approaches	■ Verbal/communication	■ Self-awareness
3. **Assessment/data gathering**—to inform, guide coaching process	■ Leadership	■ Critical thinking	■ Empathy
4. **Feedback**—to coachee, stakeholders	■ Group process	■ Strategic thinking	■ Professional credibility
5. **Goal setting and action planning**	■ Personality	■ Systems thinking	■ Adaptability/resilience
6. **Plan implementation and coaching**	■ Learning	■ Learning agility	■ Openness
7. **Evaluation of progress and reporting of results**	■ Emotional intelligence	■ Decision making	■ Self-confidence
8. **Coaching-engagement conclusion and transitioning**	■ Human development	■ Organizing, planning, project management	■ Humility
	■ Motivation	**Relational and intrapersonal**	■ Courage
	■ Organizational theory	■ Active, open listening	■ Sense of humor
	■ Cognitive behavioral psychology	■ Relationship	■ Service orientation
	■ Systems theory	■ Conflict resolution	■ Achievement orientation
	■ Social psychology	■ Process facilitation	■ Curiosity
	■ Positive psychology	■ Leadership	■ Preparedness
	Professional/business	■ Collaboration and teamwork	**Coaching-beneficial experience**
	■ Ethics, legal standards	■ Management—ambiguity, complexity, uncertainty, stress	■ Personal growth/development
	■ Business fundamentals		■ Reading/study—various disciplines
	■ Leadership development		■ Coaching supervision
	■ Process consultation		■ Varied life experiences
	■ Organization development		■ Leadership roles
	■ Cultural, geopolitical savvy		■ Working in organizations
	■ Geopolitical awareness		

Note. KSAPs = knowledge, skills, abilities, and personal characteristics. Adapted from "A Practice Analysis of Coaching Psychology: Toward a Foundational Competency Model," by V. V. Vandaveer, R. L. Lowman, K. Pearlman, and J. P. Brannick, 2016, *Consulting Psychology Journal, 68*(2), p. 139 (https://doi.org/10.1037/cpb0000057). Copyright 2016 by the American Psychological Association.

A point should be made here that there have been other efforts to study competencies important for coaching. In particular, the International Coaching Federation (ICF) has developed a widely used competency model for coaches that is available from their website (https://www.coachingfederation.org). It can be a useful summary for self-evaluation of skill areas to consider for growth, and it is used as a guide for coach training programs seeking ICF accreditation. However, their model does not include the foundational areas of evidence-based knowledge of human behavior, the nature of business economics, the political and competitive dynamics of organizations, nor the understanding of one's impact on the client's learning and development. In our view, the evidence-based knowledge required for effective leadership coaching is critically important to have and continually grow. Given our definition of coaching psychology, a more complete foundational competency model is needed, such as that displayed in Table 5.1 (Vandaveer et al., 2016).

It should be noted that no one possesses all the skills and knowledge identified by the study's respondents, and even if someone did possess them all, it would not indicate the level of their effectiveness in coaching. The CP's objective should be to acquire sufficient additional knowledge and skills in psychology areas broader than that acquired in their graduate training so that they (a) are proficient in applying different theoretical perspectives for understanding the client and (b) have a sufficiently rich repertoire of methods for helping the client achieve developmental goals (Kauffman & Hodgetts, 2016). Division 13 (Society of Consulting Psychology) and Division 14 (Society of Industrial and Organizational Psychology) of the APA offer invaluable CP workshop training at their conferences (and for CE credits for psychologists who need them). Also available are various learning opportunities on mentoring and peer supervision and consultations offered by psychologists from a variety of different psychology areas for the developing CP.

Knowledge

The SMEs and I/O and consulting psychologist respondents to the Practice Analysis Survey in the Coaching Psychology Foundational Competency

Study identified 14 psychological theoretical bases and nine professional and business knowledge areas that were most frequently named as especially important to their practice (Vandaveer et al., 2016; see Table 5.1).

As mentioned, no one is deeply versed in all these theories, nor do they have to be. However, the more the CP knows, understands, and can skillfully use, the broader and deeper their set of tools will be, the sharper their insights, and the more accurate their assessments and focus for coaching (Kauffman & Hodgetts, 2016).

Skills, Abilities, and Personal Characteristics

Table 5.1 also shows the key skills, abilities, and personal characteristics identified by SMEs as foundationally important for coaching leaders: 10 cognitive and analytical and technical skills were identified, as were nine relational (interpersonal) and intrapersonal skills and 13 personal characteristics.

Note that the first two critical relational skills listed are "active, open listening" and "relationship building and maintenance." The criticality of the quality of the coach and client relationship cannot be overstated. As the research on coaching has shown, a deep and trusting connection with the client is necessary for creating the psychologically safe environment that allows working at whatever psychological levels are necessary for achieving the goals at the (a) behavioral level—identifying the behaviors that are inhibiting goal achievement and working on substituting more effective behaviors; (b) cognitive behavioral level—determining the thoughts that precede and drive behaviors; and/or (c) subconscious level of awareness, cognition, values, beliefs, needs, and fears (causes) that motivate thoughts and behaviors, as well as other possible internal roadblocks, such as competing priorities that may be subconscious or proactively inhibit learning. It is also from the subconscious level of cognition that fresh insights come, sparked by something that someone (the CP or someone else) said or something the client has read, seen, or otherwise experienced or by reflection on any number or kinds of things that begin to connect for the client.

Remember that these are foundational knowledge, skills, abilities, and personal characteristics—they will get a CP started. Even if one were to have all these attributes (no one does or can), that would not guarantee coaching effectiveness. There is an art to coaching, just as there is with other professional roles—for instance, engineering, law, teaching, medical practice, or playing a musical instrument. One must acquire the required knowledge and skills, master the techniques, and then apply all that one knows and can do repeatedly until the practice becomes fluid, with left and right brain working in harmony, and learning and refined application are continual in every coaching engagement.

GRADUATE COURSEWORK

At present, formal training in the United States to be a CP is an ad hoc mix of online and classroom courses, certificate programs, and university courses. That will change gradually during the next decade as psychology graduate programs catch up to the realities of professional practice. This is well underway in the United Kingdom and Australia, where doctorate and master's degrees in coaching or coaching psychology have existed for years (e.g., Hult International Business School Masters in Executive Coaching, https://www.hult.edu/en/ashridge/qualifications/masters-in-executive-coaching/; the coaching unit at University of Sydney Master of Science in Coaching Psychology, https://www.sydney.edu.au/courses/courses/pc/master-of-science-in-coaching-psychology.html). Coming out of those programs, graduates can move directly into providing coaching services, just as with other professional degree programs. Coincident with the existence of those graduate courses of study in coaching in other countries, there are also levels of professional certification that set foundational requirements and allow for increased experience and continuing education to be recognized.

Although a few U.S. universities are launching graduate-degree programs (e.g., New York University MS in Executive Coaching and Organizational Consulting, https://www.sps.nyu.edu/homepage/academics/masters-degrees/ms-in-executive-coaching-and-organizational-consulting.html) in coaching or offering a coaching track within a related degree program, CPs who choose formal training must pick from a variety of options with little centralized guidance. In fact, part of the reason for writing this book is to contribute to making coaching psychology an organizing principle for serious preparation for leader and executive coaching and for graduate courses and programs to support that. Whether such programs are anchored in clinical, counseling, organizational, educational, or social psychology matters less than that they begin to appear.

Readers of this book who are in or preparing for graduate school in psychology can include electives that will best help prepare them for coaching: clinical, counseling, I/O, developmental, or social psychology, plus general business courses. Psychology graduate students will benefit from having the flexibility to write their own curriculum to sample from these domains. One-on-one helping using conversation goes back to the earliest roots of clinical psychology and is foundational to coaching. The value of courses and training in this domain cannot be underestimated. Many psychological theories of how human beings develop, grow, get stuck, and recover are directly applicable to coaching clients. These include learning theory, developmental psychology, psychodynamic theory, emotional intelligence, positive psychology, family-systems theories, and life-stage and typical developmental concepts, as well as existential, gestalt, narrative, somatic, and other perspectives (Peltier, 2010; Stout-Rostron, 2014), including, more recently, neuropsychology theory of leadership and coaching (Boyatzis & Jack, 2018; Dixit & Dixit, 2018; Rock & Page, 2009). Students will be well served to become conversant in key elements of these models as a foundation for their later practices.

In addition to formal graduate training, CPs need to build their client-interaction skills based on principles honed and refined in clinical and counseling psychology. Most programs in I/O psychology may include skill building for behavioral interviewing (selection and information gathering), and these skills are helpful as initial steps in acquiring expertise in diagnostic and developmental interviewing. However, most programs do not emphasize a one-on-one helping posture that applies findings from the common-factors research (McKenna & Davis, 2009) in clinical psychology. To general applied psychologists, it may appear to be anathema to say that CPs need some clinical psychology skills, but it is true. Acquiring those skills outside a clinical psychology graduate program typically involves postgraduate externships, CE workshops, coaching by a clinically trained CP or shadowing coaching engagements or both, and (this is important for all CPs) a good peer consultation relationship and having a CP for oneself.

Knowledge of business fundamentals is also essential for CPs. Various mini master of business administration courses have emerged to meet the needs of those in professional fields allied with business. Most business schools also offer courses in leadership, organizational structure and behavior, human resources, and other important softer skills business topics. CPs benefit from drawing on such courses to round out their graduate education. Whether with a doctorate or master's degree, emerging from graduate school with even a beginner's understanding of business and organizations (e.g., structures, functions, cultures, processes, policies) will make for a much faster career launch in consulting and coaching psychology.

FORMAL EXPERIENTIAL LEARNING

Many graduate programs in applied psychology include formal internship training. Where internships are not readily available, psychology graduate students who wish to do leadership coaching are encouraged to seek practical experience on their own—if not during graduate training, then after receiving their advanced degree. Internships in behavioral health clinics and other settings are usually required for advanced clinical and counseling graduate students. Internships in I/O psychology consulting firms, while optional, are highly recommended. In fact, we first met as interns at the same organizational psychology consulting firm while studying in different graduate I/O psychology programs. Such experiences are invaluable for all graduate students in applied areas of psychology, and this is also true for coaching psychology. Paid or unpaid, internships within organizations that provide leadership coaching services or in consulting firms that have coaching practices would significantly contribute to the education of CPs, whether from doctorate or master's programs. Second- or third-year graduate students should be encouraged and supported by their universities to seek internship opportunities, even if such experiences are not a formal requirement for graduation.

Externships within client organizations are also available. It is important to note that even if coaching opportunities are not immediately available, any job working in an organization will provide valuable experience for really understanding organizations, which is the context in which leaders must be effective. There is no substitute for the experiential value of working inside an organization before doing coaching. For example, acquiring knowledge from formal education or books about performance management systems, compensation practices, identification of management potential and successors to leader roles, the impact of culture (or of a bad boss) on one's effectiveness, and so on is not nearly as meaningful and deep as the actual experience of having a performance review, having one's pay determined by comparison with peers' assessed performance, seeing a less-qualified or less-productive peer get promoted over oneself, or feeling the impact of a bad boss on one's morale and performance. The same is true for feeling the effects of a terrific manager on one's spirit, sense of self-efficacy, and accomplishing things that are way beyond what one thought possible. Established larger consulting firms, of course, also can offer these experiences. However, if the aspiring CP joins a small, boutique consultancy or engages in independent practice fresh out of graduate training without practice experience inside an organization, one's knowledge will be purely intellectual, and a lot of valuable learning from experience will have been missed, which in turn places a limit on the CP's effectiveness.

Thus, training, as well as experience working within organizational contexts, is important for understanding and appreciating what it is like to work and be effective in an organization. The demand characteristics (i.e., what the organization requires of an individual) of the organizational environment consist of significant forces on the client's focus, thinking, and behaviors. This practical experience also makes clear the roles of line and staff positions and the responsibilities of human resources (HR) and talent management (TM)—at least in that one organization. Understanding the details of HR activities from the inside usually also includes familiarity with federal and local laws that apply to the people side of organizations, especially civil rights; fairness in hiring and promotion; matters of equity, diversity, and inclusion; and disabilities law. These may or may not play a role in leadership coaching, but they are part of the fabric of leading and managing effectively and are fundamental to how HR departments operate. In addition, experiencing from the inside how HR or TM partner and contract with consultants and CPs provides valuable perspective on the leader coaching engagement process. Of course, organizations differ in their leader development processes and policies, but having experience in one organization lays a foundation for understanding other approaches.

The combination of graduate training in psychology and associated internships should hone a diagnostic mindset that is critical to effective leader coaching. The client's expressed felt need at the start of a coaching engagement is almost never the resonant and engaging goal that ends up being worked toward, and listening, assessing, and seeing connections among a wide variety of inputs (i.e., what the client says and does and has done, what key stakeholders observe and perceive, how the client thinks) are key cognitive tasks that the CP performs throughout the coaching engagement. Continual hypothesis testing helps ensure that the CP and client explore possibilities sufficiently before making important decisions, including determining the primary development goals in coaching.

OTHER EXPERIENTIAL LEARNING

The present state of learning to be a CP is primarily an on-the-job endeavor supported by professional development. Doctoral and master's graduates in applied psychology who are interested in becoming CPs often join consulting firms. They may start out being trained to conduct middle-manager assessments and then move toward Level 1 coaching (short tutorial and feedback or development plan coaching). Providing direct service to managers in client organizations within contracted developmental programs is an excellent way to build foundational coaching skills, especially under the tutelage of experienced consultants and CPs. In a parallel model, psychology graduates are valued as resources internal to organizations, as seen in open positions requiring those degrees and skills. Often placed in HR, TM, leadership development, or organization development departments, they perform a variety of tasks that increasingly today include coaching. The internal capacity to deliver coaching services, usually Levels 1 and 2, has been steadily growing (see the report at https://www.conference-board.org/topics/executive-coaching/global-executive-coaching-survey-2018-report), and those organizations often provide coach training to bring their internal resources up to speed. (See also Frisch et al., 2012, Chapter 20.)

As leadership coaching grew rapidly in the past 20 years, many professional development courses in coaching were designed and offered. These may or may not be connected to a university but are nondegree, professional certificate courses. The best ones are highly experiential, provide foundational learning about leadership learning and development, and may have tracks for different types of coaches. Most programs seek to train all manner of coaches, often emphasizing personal and life coach training. For the developing CP, a certificate program in coaching may be a useful addition to graduate training, but care must be taken to determine the program's emphasis on organizationally sponsored leadership coaching (Frisch, 2019).

Along with the proliferation of many types of coach training, social media has fueled an explosion of online content related to coaching: blogs, webinars, podcasts, conferences, and professional forums all have used coaching as a focal topic. Again, because there are many types of coaching, aspiring and active CPs need to be discerning consumers of this content. A simple search for online content about coaching will yield thousands of suggestions, but relatively few of those focus on leadership coaching in organizational contexts. In addition to conferences and workshops from APA Divisions 13 and 14, now available online, the Institute of Coaching (https://www.instituteofcoaching.org), affiliated with Harvard Medical School, offers many opportunities for online learning about leadership coaching. Space here does not allow a comprehensive list of all relevant offerings, but much learning about coaching competencies can be had using the internet.

However graduate students or psychologists obtain coach training and early coaching experience, obtaining case supervision or peer consultation from CPs is a highly recommended way to keep learning (Carroll, 2008; Hawkins, 2014). In all the helping professions, case supervision by more senior practitioners has been a primary vehicle for ongoing learning. Modeled on that tradition, coach supervision has been used extensively outside the United States and only recently has been promoted widely here as peer consultation. There are exceptions, and I (MF) have used coach supervision for many years, both within learn-by-doing coach training programs and as a freestanding method of training newer coaches. CPs are encouraged to seek out a coaching supervisor or peer colleague the same way they might seek out an organizational mentor and build a working alliance. Contact may be on a regular or just-in-time, client-driven basis, but the value of having a confidential discussion partner and guide, especially for less experienced coaches, is clear. In addition to the traditional one-on-one coach supervision model, other learning structures can be applied. Peer consultation (Rego et al., 2015) in the form of small-group continuous learning sessions has been found to be helpful for CPs in mid-career and later for continuing to learn and enhance their expertise. One model that I (VV) have found to be particularly well received is bringing together a small group of CPs whose psychology backgrounds are different (e.g., I/O, clinical, counseling, developmental, social, neuropsychology) and analyzing together each other's most challenging cases. The learning from insights that CPs from different areas of psychology have with respect to a given case enhances everyone's learning and ongoing growth.

Another approach is the formation of support subgroups among cohorts of people who graduate from coach training programs because they often maintain contact with each other and form long-standing close relationships. The usual confidentiality rules apply, and CPs can shield client names and employers while getting feedback, ideas, and suggestions from peer coaches. Whether with an individual case supervisor or peer coaches, CPs can benefit from others' perspectives and take part in a time-honored tradition in the ongoing development of helping professionals.

As with any practice-driven professional service that is relatively new, self-taught practitioners lead by example. They take learning from related fields and organize it under the emerging practice area and build from there. Professional journals and books may document those innovations and enhance the appeal. A few scattered outposts of training may come and go, and then practice standards begin to formalize. For most practice changes, that's as far as things go, and that's where we were in U.S. coaching in the early 2000s. Coaching, however, was one of those professional service areas that grew and spread rapidly, reminiscent of the human relations movement in management in the 1950s and the rise of positive psychology in the 1980s. And although we could argue that psychologists' use of the term *executive coaching* predates all other uses of the term in the United States, coaching has grown beyond any specific field and sprouted in many helping interactions and professions. This has normalized one-on-one helping, but at the same time, it has confused what is meant by the term *executive coaching*. Psychologists seeking training toward becoming a CP for executives must make sure that selected coach training is focused on organizationally sponsored coaching.

Achieving expertise mastery in coaching requires constant work on the primary tool for executive coaching psychology: one's self. Continuing to learn—from a wide variety of sources and experiences—is essential to effective practice in coaching psychology.

This chapter has focused on how to prepare oneself to do leadership coaching for executives and leaders. The suggestions presented here will help get one started. Once one has begun to provide coaching psychology services, ongoing learning, growing, and expanding one's repertoire of skills will be essential to increasing effectiveness, and development will include more and more about developing the art of coaching psychology. Being strong in many foundational competencies is truly only the foundation: It represents the "table stakes" for practicing coaching psychology. What makes the difference between mediocre and truly masterful coaching is in the how—how one uses all those competencies in combination with who they are as a person: the self.

Growing one's expertise and continually working toward professional mastery is a lifelong journey. Just a few examples of what one can do to constantly hone, sharpen, and refine the primary coaching tool are the following:

- Keep abreast of the emerging science—in all the related fields of psychology, neuroscience, adult development, and learning and organization development, as well as in anything pertaining to the assessment tools and strategies one uses.
- Keep abreast of current events in the business sectors you serve, as well as emerging trends in management and relevant technology.
- Enroll in relevant CE workshops—primarily at psychology professional conferences, such as the Society of Consulting Psychology (APA Division 13) and the Society for Industrial and Organizational Psychology (APA Division 14).
- Obtain feedback from coaching clients—the coaching client, that person's manager, and coaching sponsors. Use that information to continue to grow, figure out how to leverage the areas of perceived great strengths, and then work on the areas that can be improved.
- Engage in peer consultation. Review cases, situations, and client feedback with a trusted peer-CP. The value of peer consultation cannot be overstated (Rousmaniere et al., 2017). The mutual learning that occurs is hugely beneficial, and the mutual support between colleagues is invaluable. Peer-consultation small groups composed of psychologists from different areas of psychology provide particularly powerful learning and support experiences. Note that our international coaching psychology colleagues refer to this as *coach supervision*. We prefer *peer consultation* as the more fitting term.
- Keep a journal of coaching experiences and learnings, and periodically review and reflect. Doing this will surface additional insights that are helpful catalysts to the development of mastery in coaching psychology.
- Give back to our discipline by writing, sharing learnings and insights from experience. The connections (worldwide) that that brings, as well as the learnings and wisdom of colleagues all over the world it promotes, will also catalyze further insights and advancement toward professional mastery.

- Reflect on and extract metaphors and learnings from life experiences to foster insight with clients and enrich your learning as you continue to build mastery in coaching psychology.

By way of example, my (VV's) path to executive coaching from doctoral training in an I/O psychology program that emphasized (a) the quantitative research side of I/O, job analysis, test development and validation, applied organizational research, and individual assessment and (b) social-organizational, organization development, motivation, cognitive psychology, and leadership theories has been a personally and professionally rewarding experience.

My route from predicting an individual's likely success in a leadership role to helping leaders be more effective, working one-on-one, began with an organizational transformation consultation to the top management of a large public company and an associated job analysis of all jobs top to bottom. The identified most important competencies at the senior management level were different in a few but important ways, and debriefs of the job and role analyses with the top executives led to requested individual consultations to help them elevate and hone their leadership effectiveness (years later called leadership or executive coaching). Executive coaching became an increasingly larger part of my professional practice over time. My I/O training was a good foundation but was inadequate for maximum effectiveness in leader coaching (as is true for every graduate program in psychology).

Initially, my method of coaching was "OD facilitation one on one," and my work to build executive coaching proficiency involved learning from clinical and counseling psychologists, management and business school luminaries, sociologists, and cultural anthropologists and the rich experience of coaching many leaders, including internationally and cross-culturally. Most notably, early on, a 3-day course at the Gestalt Institute of Cleveland, in which I had hurriedly enrolled for a final three CE credits I needed by the following Monday (for psychology license renewal), was foundational and instrumental in me making the shift from predicting leader effectiveness to helping leaders develop.

That gestalt organization system development program was a peak and pivotal experience that shattered my nomothetic paradigm for use in one-on-one helping work, challenged "noble truths" learned well in grad school, uncovered blind spots, and helped me "stop tripping over my *p* values" (probability of a significant effect in large-sample statistical analyses). The lessons were hard and uncomfortable. But I needed three more CE credits, so I stayed to the end. By the end, I was doing some serious self-reflection, listening in a way that I hadn't before (because it was too personal), and letting go of some of my rigidity about statistical reliability and validity applied to a one-on-one helping relationship. What I experienced that weekend was expert Gestalt CPs connecting with me, helping me really hear and accept as good data what an individual says, data that need to be interpreted by an effective partnership with the client, engaged in joint meaning making. It was the beginning of a whole new phase of my development journey—both professionally and personally. My practice today is enriched by the combination of nomothetic and idiographic assessment (see footnote 1 on p. 118), a mixture of qualitative and quantitative approaches. Executive coaching is a natural fit with my "helping" orientation and is a primary source of my learning and professional fulfillment.

The following is another example, this time of a clinician's path to adding coaching to his professional activities:

> Chris had graduated from a respected clinical psychology program and had the good fortune to intern at an active and successful clinic in New York City. After getting his degree, he accepted a full-time position with the clinic and was supervised by the well-known directors of the clinic. He took to the work, his patient load grew, and with the blessings of the clinic, within a few years, he opened his own practice. This also built quickly to the point where he was managing the flow of patients of clinicians working for him. That part of being a manager was fine with him; what wasn't fine was the newly controlling and intrusive role of insurance companies in psychotherapy. The administrative burden did not play to his clinical strengths, and the second-guessing did not align with his confident and direct

personality. At this major frustration point in his career, Chris noticed an ad in the *APA Monitor* looking for psychologists to staff assessment centers run by an applied psychology consulting firm. While this was a completely unknown professional activity, he found that he enjoyed it and that the business case studies of the assessment centers taught him a lot about business organizations, structure, roles, and leadership.

This firm also provided leadership coaching to clients, and Chris was particularly drawn to adding that to his growing assessment skills. He joined APA Divisions 13 and 14, as well as local chapters of HR and (leadership development) professional organizations. As a focused and determined person, he read books and took courses on coaching and was given opportunities to both assess and provide feedback to assessment center participants. There were certainly challenges in juggling the different demands and standards of the two roles, clinical and coaching, but he consciously navigated those differences so that he could switch "hats" during a workday or week. Chris has continued to be successful on both fronts, and he now does more leadership coaching than clinical work, but his practice will always include both sets of services.

SUMMARY

This chapter has provided many specific suggestions based on the principle that there is no single path to becoming a CP. There are many options and alternatives in building competence beyond advanced degree programs and, of course, in the application of those competencies. Individuals who are self-monitoring, self-reflective, and self-developing will advance their professional growth faster with the support of a supervisory-mentoring or peer-consultative relationship. A classic and valuable book on the general challenges of putting theory into professional practice and building consulting expertise is Argyris and Schön (1974), and there are several useful handbooks on coaching in organizations (Cox et al., 2014; Passmore et al., 2013; Riddle et al., 2015; Scott & Reynolds, 2010; Stout-Rostron, 2014).

6

Ethical and Professional Issues in Coaching Psychology

For U.S. psychologists in all areas of specialization and psychology graduate students, the *Ethical Principles of Psychologists and Code of Conduct* of the American Psychological Association (APA; i.e., the APA Ethics Code; 2017) is the foundation for guidance about professional and ethical conduct. The APA Ethics Code has had several updates and refinements over the years, and at this writing, it is undergoing yet another update. Coaching psychologists (CPs) should become familiar with the latest version of the APA Ethics Code and the case examples provided in other texts and ethics courses. The workshops provided for CE credit by the Society of Consulting Psychology, the Society for Industrial and Organizational Psychology, and APA are particularly helpful for learning about the professional and ethical challenges and dilemmas that happen when working in or consulting to organizations, as well as the ethical principles and standards that apply. Case studies shared are typically the

https://doi.org/10.1037/0000293-007
Coaching Psychology: Catalyzing Excellence in Organizational Leadership, by V. V. Vandaveer and M. H. Frisch

participants' own (Lowman & Cooper, 2018). A (free) copy of the current APA Ethics Code can be downloaded from the APA website at https://www.apa.org/ethics/code. At this writing, the 2017 version is the latest, and the following descriptions and case vignettes are based on it. We recommend accessing it for easy reference as you read this chapter.

The APA Ethics Code is composed of (a) general principles and (b) ethical standards. The five general principles are aspirational in nature, and "their intent is to guide and inspire psychologists toward the highest ethical ideals of the profession" (APA, 2017, General Principles section, para. 1). The ethical standards are enforceable rules (by state licensing boards) for the conduct of psychologists (APA, 2017, Introduction and Applicability section, para. 1).

GENERAL PRINCIPLES

The following is a summary of the General Principles of the APA Ethics Code. The descriptions are excerpted from the full text.

- Principle A: Beneficence and Nonmaleficence. "Psychologists strive to benefit those with whom they work and take care to do no harm" (APA, 2017, General Principles section, para. 2).
- Principle B: Fidelity and Responsibility. "Psychologists establish relationships of trust with those with whom they work [clients]" (APA, 2017, General Principles section, para. 3).
- Principle C: Integrity. "Psychologists seek to promote accuracy, honesty, and truthfulness in the science, teaching, and practice of psychology" (APA, 2017, General Principles section, para. 4).
- Principle D: Justice. "Psychologists exercise reasonable judgment and take precautions to ensure that their potential biases, the boundaries of their competence, and the limitations of their expertise do not lead to nor condone unjust practices" (APA, 2017, General Principles section, para. 5).
- Principle E: Respect for People's Rights and Dignity. "Psychologists respect the dignity and worth of all people, and the rights of individuals to privacy, confidentiality, and self-determination" (APA, 2017, General Principles section, para. 6).

ETHICAL STANDARDS

As mentioned previously, the ethical standards that apply to psychologists are enforceable by state licensing boards. Although addressing each of the standards is beyond the scope of this book, we have selected eight standards for elaboration, with case vignettes included to illustrate their application in the practice of coaching psychology. Possible responses to the ethical dilemmas posed by the cases are suggested.

Misuse of Psychologists' Work (Standard 1.01) and Maintaining Confidentiality (Standard 4.01)

As with anything a CP undertakes for a client, it is necessary to "begin with the end in mind," including what will happen after the coaching ends. Per the APA Ethics Code, we are responsible for preventing the misuse of our work—during and after the coaching or consulting engagement. Thus, for example, in the contracting phase of a coaching engagement, agreement is reached on such matters as (a) the nature and extent of confidentiality (e.g., specifically who will—and will not—have access to these reports and the information contained in them), (b) who (what role) shall be responsible for the ongoing safekeeping and ensuring adherence to the contract agreements, and (c) the "expiration date" of assessment reports, at which time the reports will be shredded as expired confidential documents. It is important that the CP and client implement specific safeguards to ensure the ongoing upholding of the contract agreements.

Consider the following scenario. Suppose the CP and a client have agreed in the contracting phase that only the coaching client's manager and the talent management (TM) representative responsible for the individual's executive development will see the assessment report and other reports produced in the coaching engagement. How can the CP be assured that that agreement will be adhered to after the engagement has ended?

What if the manager retires and the client gets a new manager? Will that person, not having been part of the conversations in contracting, understand the importance of the confidentiality of the material and uphold the agreement?

What if the TM representative receives a promotion and her direct report now takes responsibility for upholding the agreements—and also now has access? In this case, a competent TM leader will likely orient and mentor their replacement well, and the commitment to the contract will be continued. However, that may not be the case, and the coach (and the coach's client) may never know about the change.

What if the client, partly or largely as an outcome of the CP's coaching, was identified as having high potential for moving up in the levels of leadership, and 3 years later, the client is being considered for a big promotion into a position in a different part of the large company? If the hiring executive requests to see the individual's assessment report and profile from 3 years previous, should the current manager and/or human resources (HR) or TM representative responsible for its safekeeping turn it over? And what if the hiring executive keeps a copy of it? What happens then if information in the report is misinterpreted and, on the basis of that interpretation, the decision to hire or promote the individual is rescinded? How can the CP possibly be responsible for what happens 3 years later? The CP has no control over what happens after they are gone. Could the CP possibly be charged with an ethics violation for this outcome? Although the likelihood of that happening is small, it is possible. Therefore, CPs must anticipate—and take steps to prevent—such misuse of assessment information obtained during coaching.

Suppose, in contrast, proper protocols had been in place, and someone (e.g., the TM representative) who had been trained to understand the CP's reports, instead of handing over the report to the hiring executive, met with the new manager to go through the report to ensure accurate understanding of what the report was saying. The client might have been promoted into a position of greater responsibility and impact, which in turn, may have brought many more opportunities with even greater impact and higher salaries. Such reports should have a specified "shelf life" (in our practices, 3 to maximum 5 years), after which time they will be destroyed as other confidential documents are.

In this example, in 3 years, someone working on their continued development could have made significant progress such that the client's

3-year-old profile no longer accurately reflects their current level of leader effectiveness. It is also the case that over time, some abilities decrease; therefore, it is rarely appropriate to rely on outdated reports.

In the initial contracting phase of a coaching engagement, in addition to agreements to the confidentiality of sensitive information, there also needs to be a specification of (a) how the sensitive information will be handled, (b) who else will have ongoing access, and (c) how the agreement will be upheld in perpetuity.

In leadership coaching, it is typically the case that the client's manager and perhaps a TM representative may have access to summary assessment information (e.g., an executive summary report) that the coach and client release, and also the shared development plan, but not specific assessment scale scores nor computer-generated assessment reports. If assessments are to be for both development and as input to selection/promotion decisions, then that needs to be explicitly stated in contracting; and management needs to understand that the dual purpose could possibly affect the client's responses on the self-report inventories. The psychometrically skilled CP can help mitigate the risk of an inaccurate "read" of the client by "triangulating" results in a carefully selected battery of assessments and a high-quality cognitive-behavioral interview.

The CP needs to work with the TM or other appropriate representative to set up the (fail-safe) safeguards even before coaching begins. If the company does not have a TM or formal HR function, some other function (not individual—because individuals move, get promoted, retire, or otherwise leave the organization) can be made responsible (e.g., legal or administration). Another option is for the CP to keep the information secure and only make it available to those who have a need to know, in a manner consistent with the provisions of the agreement. The CP needs to decide how long assessment information should be kept, considering a number of factors including (but not limited to) professional "best practices" standards or guidelines, the assessment evidence base at the time (i.e., research on the different types of assessment regarding "recommended shelf life" and psychometric properties of the particular assessments—e.g., reliability, fakeability). Whatever retention period is specified, the designated keeper of the confidential reports (e.g., TM, HR, other designated function) is responsible for annually purging assessment reports that are more than 3 to 5 years old.

Another important assessment security safeguard is to be careful about sending an assessment report by email and particularly when sending a report to a workplace email address (inquire whether the client organization has specific secure confidentiality safeguards in their email system— e.g., for some companies if "confidential" is the first word in the subject line, the email will only go to the target individual, and no one else would have access). If a client requests a soft copy of an assessment report, it is typical that the document is emailed to a private email address and be password protected.

Conflicts Between Ethics and Organizational Demands (Standard 1.03)

According to Standard 1.03 of the APA Ethics Code,

> If the demands of an organization with which psychologists are affiliated or for whom they are working are in conflict with this Ethics Code, psychologists clarify the nature of the conflict, make known their commitment to the Ethics Code, and take reasonable steps to resolve the conflict consistent with the General Principles and Ethical Standards of the Ethics Code.

Be advised that while many of these ethical principles and standards may seem obvious, and the reader may well feel, "Of course, I would do that anyway" or "I would never do that," in actual professional practice, ethical dilemmas and/or challenges occur all the time. The CP must be able to recognize them immediately when they occur so that the appropriate steps can be taken to prevent or address the situation in a timely manner.

Consider the following coaching situation. The HR vice president (VP) of a recently merged midsized public company called in a CP with whom he had worked when he had been in a similar role at a previous company. He stated that the new CEO would like to meet with the CP to discuss doing assessments of the executive team like those that had been done at the VP's previous company. He had shown the CEO his assessment report and computer-generated assessment profiles (i.e., interpretations and graphic displays of the results on each attribute assessed) and relayed that the CEO was "very interested in having that done here."

The new CEO, Frederick, had a strong finance background and significant experience with mergers and acquisitions. The board of directors had selected him to be CEO of the merged company to assure that the merger would work and become profitable quickly.

The CP met with Frederick to discuss his interest in doing assessments of his executive team and to understand the intended purpose. Regarding the purpose, Frederick said, "I just want to know my team." He wanted psychological assessments on his executive team members; the information was to be only for him. He would see the profiles and reports, but his team members would not see their profiles.

What would you do in this situation? This is how the CP handled this request: The CP diplomatically explained that requiring the direct reports to take an assessment that would only be seen by their CEO would make everyone apprehensive and would affect the reliability and validity of the assessment results because the assessments were mostly self-report inventories. The CP explained that if those assessed would not get to see the results, many would likely be cautious in responding, tending to answer as they thought they "should" rather than as they truly see themselves, thus resulting in a normatively interpreted profile that would likely not be a true picture. And worse, that would stimulate apprehension and create mistrust between the CEO and his team (the opposite of what he needed to be doing—building a strong, cohesive, high-performing executive team). The CP suggested that Frederick consider having the assessments be part of individual and team development (as they were in the HR VP's previous company). Each individual would receive feedback on their own results, and the whole team (with written permission from each team member) would see the profiles plotted together so that all could better understand each other to be more effective in leading together. (Note that the assessments to be used were designed for team development purposes.) To this suggestion, Frederick said, "Maybe later. Right now, all I want is the assessments." The CP did not try to persuade the CEO otherwise because his mind was made up, and he was the potential client. However, the CP politely explained that she could not conduct the assessments under the conditions he required because used in that way, the assessments could have the opposite effect of what he wanted, which is to know his team better and build a stronger team to achieve his and the board's bold goals, and ethically the CP was committed to "do no harm." Unless the assessment process would benefit direct reports as well as the CEO and the organization, the CP could not comply with Frederick's request, in keeping with the APA Ethics Code, which requires that CPs do their best to avoid harming individuals and companies, especially when that harm is avoidable and preventable.

Note that the APA Ethics Code does not say "do no harm" (see Standard 3.04a): "Psychologists take reasonable steps to avoid harming their clients/patients, students, supervisees, research participants, organizational clients, and others with whom they work, and to minimize harm where it is foreseeable and unavoidable." However, nonpsychologist clients understand the intent not to do harm. An example of a kind of "harm" that happens is in the selection of employees for a job. Someone does not get the job—and often, many people don't get the job. Only one person is selected. That may impact some of the applicants financially as well as emotionally. If part of the selection decision process involved psychological testing by a CP, the CP must ensure that they are competent to be doing assessments for use in making employment decisions—both technically (psychometrics) and understanding and complying with the applicable laws and statutes and federal testing guidelines with respect to Equal Employment Opportunity.

Sometimes the CP just needs to walk away (even, by the way, if they need the work).

A postscript to the case vignette is that, eventually, the CEO agreed to engage in executive team development, which would include individual and team assessments, and he agreed to the conditions (i.e., that individuals would see their own results and—with written permission from everyone—would see each other's profiles), which enhanced understanding and contributed to building a stronger team. The VP of HR was the one who persuaded him that that was the right thing to do.

Multiple Relationships (Standard 3.05)

Organizationally sponsored leadership coaching goes beyond the dyad of the coach and client; there are always multiple relationships that a coach has in the client's organization, as described in Chapter 2. The APA Ethics Code identifies multiple relationships as needing special attention to avoid ethical conflicts. See Standard 3.05 in the APA Ethics Code.

The most recent updates to the APA Ethics Code (2017), acknowledging that general applied psychologists are often expected (even required sometimes) to socialize with clients, included the following helpful addendum:

> A psychologist refrains from entering into a multiple relationship if the multiple relationship could reasonably be expected to impair the psychologist's objectivity, competence, or effectiveness in performing his or her functions as a psychologist, or otherwise risks exploitation or harm to the person with whom the professional relationship exists. Multiple relationships that would not reasonably be expected to cause impairment or risk exploitation or harm are not unethical. (Standard 3.05, Multiple Relationships, para. 2)

Note that it is incumbent on the CP to ensure that they maintain their independence in the coaching relationship because the quality of their work and the benefit to the client depends on it. In the contracting phase of the coaching engagement, it is important that the CP specify who their clients are (e.g., the coaching client, the manager, and, if applicable, the HR or TM sponsor as well as the organization as a whole) and also the nature and extent of confidentiality with each client.

One scenario in which the coaching or consulting psychologist frequently engages in social activities with members of the client organization is in international work. There are many countries in which socializing is expected and is the norm. The psychologist must be vigilant in ensuring that they maintain their objectivity with—and therefore, value for—the client.

Psychological Services Delivered to or Through Organizations (Standard 3.11)

Particularly pertinent to coaching psychology as a subset of consulting psychology is Standard 3.11, which specifies what the psychologist needs to do in the contracting phase of the coaching (or consulting) to ensure mutual understanding and agreement about the services to be performed. We encourage you to read this standard now (in the 2017 APA Ethics Code document or the updated version that replaces it).

Transparency from the beginning and throughout the engagement— and faithfully upholding agreed rules of engagement—will contribute to building and maintaining trusting relationships with each of the various clients, and it will help ensure that there will be no misunderstandings later about who will (and will not) see what and when. That transparency should also extend to any past relationships that the coach has had with the organization. The names of past clients in the organization need not be revealed, but the coach's past learning about the organization is often a credibility builder for new coaching clients.

If multiple people within a reporting structure will be receiving coaching, it is important that individuals be given the choice of having the same CP as other colleagues or someone different. Some individuals may prefer to have a CP who is not working with their colleagues, especially if they are concerned about confidentiality. Others prefer that the same CP work with everyone. This is often true when the CP is working with the leadership team as a whole. Preferences generally reflect characteristics of the culture (e.g., general level of trust) and personal experience with prior consultants who promised confidentiality and broke their promise. Honoring clients' preferences is important for the building of trust and strong relationships.

CPs who work at the senior levels of organizations may need to maintain their focus primarily at those levels. Their relationships at the top may preclude their working directly with individuals at levels below the senior team because of natural concerns about what the CP might say to those in power above them. It is best if CPs recognize this inherent conflict and do not range vertically in promoting their coaching within the organization. In addition, clients themselves are unlikely to feel safe enough to voice concerns about being coached by the CEO's coach, and they need to not be put in that position. The CP needs to recognize that those individuals need different CPs, always putting the welfare of the client ahead of one's business considerations.

Conflict of Interest (Standard 3.06)

Standard 3.06 of the APA Ethics Code pertains to the need to avoid conflicts of interest to ensure avoidance of anything that might—or might be perceived to—impair their objectivity. For CPs, examples of a conflict include the following:

- providing coaching services to a company in which the CP's spouse is a high-level executive—it goes without saying (but we'll say it anyway) that no one will trust that their confidences are kept from management;
- providing leadership coaching and making the decision to have a close personal relationship with one of the coaching clients—or their manager (dual relationship; see APA Ethics Code Standard 10.08); and
- owning or trading client company's stock while working with members of the top management team, in which case the CP may be (or be perceived to be) privy to information that the public does not yet know. If one does own the client company's stock, it is highly advisable that the CP has nothing to do with trading that stock either way (buying or selling) while engaged to provide professional coaching services.

The best way to ensure that no conflicts of interest exist in such situations is to divest oneself of any financial connections to the client and the sponsoring organization that could conceivably be viewed as a clear conflict of interest. An example of a scenario that would likely not be viewed as a conflict is that in which the CP owns stock in a mutual fund managed by someone else. Analogously, in coaching within not-for-profit organizations, coaches who feel aligned with their organizational values and mission must be careful; it is critical to know where to draw the line between coaching and attempting to influence decisions or courses of action. Whether through overidentification with the mission or the coach's stock holdings, it is important to avoid distractions from a truly client-centered focus on the CP's mission: facilitating learning and development of the leader. The CP must always be keenly aware of—and keep true to—the CP role as coach, advisor, and facilitator and not a participant in decision making.

It may feel like a stretch to think that stock price may be influenced by what happens in a coaching relationship or that a coach's interactions with a client could be constrained by share price concerns until one considers that coaches do engage at the highest organizational levels. Specific behavior that emerges from a high-level coaching relationship may, in fact, have high visibility through CEO presentations or other public relations efforts. And, of course, one would expect broad organizational impact and value as a result of changes in the client's leadership behavior related to developmental coaching because that is the purpose of coaching high-level leaders—improving their effectiveness because of their influence on a large number of people. In Level 4 advisory consultation, the trusted leadership advisor role (Wasylyshyn, 2015), the CP works with the client-led agenda. When the executive client is using the CP as a sounding board for thinking through prospective major decisions, it is important that the CP remain firmly in the facilitating thinking model. It is a tightrope to walk; facilitating thinking can easily be done in a subtle manner that nudges the client in a certain direction. Being a thought partner is invaluable to the top executives, especially when the CP has the wisdom and seasoning required to facilitate the client's thinking through all angles while remaining neutral oneself about the issue (Welsh et al., 2015).

Boundaries of Competence (Standard 2.01)

While it seems like a "no-brainer" that CPs must be sure to not practice outside their boundaries of competence, individual CPs are not always cognizant of what those boundaries are. It is critically important to actively work to identify those boundaries, including working to understand the significant differences between coaching psychology (executive and leader development coaching) and (a) clinical or counseling therapy and (b) organization development and to have a good understanding of the limits of competence relative to the coaching approach and knowledge (including social-organizational context) and skills required and knowledge and skill in working with individuals of different ethnic, cultural, gender, and age characteristics.

Clinical and counseling psychologists who work with organizational leaders in therapy may be unsure how leadership coaching is different from individual therapy. Further, based on the descriptions in Chapter 1, the differences primarily include (a) focus (leadership effectiveness in organizational context); (b) the organizational context (social-psychological and power dynamics and the client's business world); (c) as much or more attention to the client's strengths as a leader as to their development needs, helping the client figure out how to even better leverage those strengths; and (d) should clinical therapy be needed, referring the client to a qualified professional outside the organization.

The CP needs to have been well trained in the key context-related factors, such as organizational power dynamics; leadership and organizational structure, processes, and functioning; nature of performance expectations and accountability requirements; individuals' responses to the demand characteristics of their role in context; and the social psychology of organizations—just to name a few of the more obvious factors. CPs skilled in family therapy will see similarities between family dynamics and leadership team dynamics and assume they are similar enough that they can automatically be effective in working with a leadership team. They are, of course, different in the nature of team member relationships, the nature of interaction dynamics, and the social psychology of the organizational culture (Katz & Kahn, 1978). Just to name a few of the differences: Team members are all adults, and the focus of leader development coaching is different from that of a team in group therapy or working with an emotionally distressed family. In addition, clients of internal CPs may also be colleagues who (particularly in Western societies) may be competing for organizational rewards. Each team member responds to the demand characteristics of their role and culture, and people respond differently to the political and power dynamics. A CP who is not well versed in organizational psychology, business, and working with leadership teams will find it hard to maintain credibility and effectiveness.

It is always important to be keenly aware of what you know, what you do not know, and what you need to know to ensure that you are working within your boundaries of competence with respect to working with leaders in organizations.

In the contracting phase of coaching, the CP makes sure they are well equipped to work with individuals from the target populations to receive leader coaching, and if they are not, they must (if they know one or more people who are well equipped) refer the organization to a more appropriate CP. In any case, the CP must be prepared to decline the coaching engagement.

Knowledge and expertise relative to cross-cultural issues in coaching psychology are especially important, as is keeping up-to-date with evolving understanding from research and practice. Many states currently require a certain number of CE credits in cultural diversity and cross-cultural issues each year for license renewal. Although sufficient attention to this topic is beyond the scope of this book, there are many good references for CPs. For starters, see Coultas et al. (2011), Hofstede (2001), House et al. (2004), Lowman (2007), Passmore (2013), Peterson (2007), Rosinski (2003), Roth (2017), Stout-Rostron et al. (2014), and Vandaveer (2012a).

Examples include an executive from an organization's home country struggling to transition into the American branch of that organization or an American executive transferred overseas navigating both country and organizational culture differences. CPs in these situations need experience and expertise in cross-cultural issues, especially tied to the specific country cultures involved.

Maintaining Competence (Standard 2.03)

Standard 2.03 on maintaining competence should be read closely. As mentioned in the suggestions in Chapter 5 about how to prepare for becoming a CP, it is important that the CP knows what they know and what they don't; CPs must be aware of the limits of their competence and stay within those limits. Failure to stay within one's areas of competence could, in the worst case, cause unintended harm to the client, including possibly the client organization, or, in a less severe case, deliver a suboptimal developmental coaching experience to the client.

Particular attention should be given to special segments of the population, such as race, age, and culture, in the contracting phase of a coaching engagement. When coaching someone distinctly different from themself, it will be important that the CP know their competence level for being effective with that individual. It is also highly advisable that CPs get continuing education regularly in ethics and cultural issues, keeping current with changes in society, the law, and the world.

As covered in Chapter 5, starting with Level 1 and Level 2 coaching, then continuing to build expertise through workshops led by experts in areas related to coaching and working with a highly skilled CP mentor is the best way to build expertise toward eventual Level 3 coaching and Level 4 advisory consultation. Clinical and counseling psychologists too often assume that they need no additional training to do coaching, and they bring their clinical therapy skills and methods into organizations— doing what they have always done but calling it *coaching* instead of *therapy* or *counseling*. Often, those engagements don't last long, as discussed in Chapter 2.

Industrial and organizational (I/O) psychologists may have an even tougher time than clinicians when migrating their professional practice into executive coaching. It is a difficult transition to let go of one's *p* values and an almost insatiable need to quantify everything and one's discomfort with the role of "primary instrument for change." That is getting much too personal for many I/O psychologists! Often, they are comfortable enough with the science that underlies coaching but are uneasy with the art required (characterized in part by a deep connection with the individual) to be effective in facilitating learning in another person.

Gaining and maintaining competence in coaching psychology is a lifelong journey. Achieving expertise mastery in coaching psychology is a worthy aspirational goal, and once having achieved that status as acknowledged by professional peers and clients, the learning journey continues. The world of work and organizations is continuously evolving. For example, at the time of this writing, leadership and coaching of leaders are changing quite significantly in response to rapid developments in technology and a global pandemic.

Privacy and Confidentiality (Standard 4)

For CPs, it is important to specify at the outset the nature and limits of confidentiality, including clarifying in writing what kind of information will be kept strictly between the coaching client and the CP, what information will be provided to the coaching client's manager and (if applicable) other coaching sponsors, as well as under what conditions or circumstances another manager may see the executive summary of the individual's assessment report. Once the manager and sponsors sign their agreement to the terms of the coaching engagement contract, the CP must abide by that confidentiality agreement fully and unconditionally. (See APA Ethics Code Standard 4.02, Discussing the Limits of Confidentiality.)

An exception to the confidentiality rule is the unlikely event that not sharing the information might result in harm to the client or others. Note that, occasionally, a sponsor (typically, the primary client who is the coaching client's manager) makes requests for information inconsistent with usual professional practice and standards—for example, with respect to confidentiality. When this happens, the CP will need to explain why confidentiality in the coaching process is necessary for achieving the desired outcomes and to obtain agreement among all parties before commencing with coaching—during the contracting phase—to avoid serious difficulties later in the process.

Missteps in handling confidentiality can create major breaches in coaching relationships. Case examples often focus on a coach sharing too much with sponsors or answering inappropriate questions about promotability or other organizational decisions (Lowman, 1998). Therefore, as suggested by Standard 4.01, CPs must have a clear grasp of (a) what is confidential and what is not, (b) challenges to confidentiality they may experience, and, most important, (c) self-awareness about their motivations or emotions that may render them blind to potential breaches of confidentiality. Examples include concerns about future projects, wanting to be accommodating or liked, and intimidation by organizational authority or power, all of which are certainly vulnerabilities that CPs need to be aware of and have active strategies to blunt, even at the risk of displeasing a coaching sponsor. Although examples often focus on external coaches, internal coaches may have greater challenges in maintaining confidentiality because of likely informal interactions with sponsors and the consequent multiple roles they play in the organization.

An example of the latter is serving simultaneously as an internal coach and member of the succession planning review team. Having in-depth and confidential information about a subset of high-potential candidates being reviewed builds in bias (either for or against). In addition, relaying one's knowledge of those candidates betrays the confidentiality promised to the coaching clients and also affects the less-known candidates' standing in the review. There are always diplomatic ways to deflect inappropriate inquiries; however, if the CP has done proper contracting in the beginning—and avoids being in dual roles that set up inherent conflict—the instances of that happening will be few to none. CPs need to recognize a challenge to promised confidentiality and always be ready with rehearsed options for handling it while maintaining confidentiality with the client.

Early-career psychologists should note that it is important that CPs be squeaky clean in keeping confidentiality commitments. This is one key attribute that differentiates CPs from the many consultants and coaches in the world who easily promise confidentiality then fail to keep their commitment. Unfortunately, occasionally a CP will find a client organization whose leaders have been burned before and do not trust anyone's promise of confidentiality. In those cases, it may take a little longer to gain that client's trust, but the CP's reputation will follow them. And if the CP models what keeping confidences looks like, they can be assured that word will get around. Of course, the reverse is also true: Once confidence is broken, it is almost unbelievable how fast that word gets around—and not only in the client organization where one slipped; other prospective client organizations will hear about it as well.

PROFESSIONAL ISSUES IN COACHING PSYCHOLOGY

Professional issues are challenges of an ethical or moral nature and/or that are otherwise problematic that can arise in a coaching and/or consulting engagement. Examples of a moral issue might be when a client asks the CP to lie to their manager about them or do something that would violate the contract. An example of an "otherwise problematic" type of professional issue is a "surprise" of some kind that impacts the CP–client coaching work (e.g., a big organizational change, such as a reduction in workforce or executive and board decision to spin off the part of the business in which the client works and sell it to a much larger company, raising a lot of uncertainty and ambiguity for the client and CP).

Disingenuousness in the Coaching Process

Consider this scenario:

> A CP was engaged to coach a senior-level executive (Tom) in a large international manufacturing public company. The CP had been referred to Tom's new manager by the company's head of TM. Tom had been the heir apparent to succeed in one of the chief executive level roles when the incumbent retired. However, when the retirement was announced, to everyone's surprise, a woman (Katherine), and not Tom, was named the successor. Katherine was smart and accomplished but had nowhere near the knowledge and skills, achievements, experience, internal and external connections, and gravitas that Tom had. Everyone was shocked that Tom was not selected. Tom, who had been groomed by the incumbent in that role to succeed him, was stunned—and devastated. He now would be reporting to Katherine!
>
> The CP's first meeting with Katherine to discuss the coaching engagement was in the large board room. The TM person (the contact

client) introduced the CP to Katherine (a primary client) and hurriedly left. The meeting with Katherine was strange; a lawyer from the legal department was also present and was taking copious notes on a laptop while Katherine and the CP discussed Tom's development needs. The CP inquired about the purpose of the note taking. Katherine's response was, "Oh, I document everything. Don't worry, our conversation is confidential." Katherine described Tom's problematic behavior that had to change as insubordination. He had expected that he would be selected for her role, and now he found himself in an awkward position; on top of that, everyone looked to him for information, input, and advice.

Katherine appeared to lack warmth, was rather prickly, and was dismissive of Tom, and she had not attempted to win him over and build their relationship. Further, she had demoted him with no warning. Then Katherine had "provided him with a coach" (whom she arranged for the TM representative to find) for the purpose of "fixing his attitude." The CP's first inclination was to decline the coaching engagement because the potential coaching client's manager did not appear supportive of Tom and his development; the constant presence of the lawyer typing notes about the CP's and Katherine's conversation was certainly suggestive of a legal case being prepared against Tom. The CP's second thought, however, was that it might be important to take on the coaching engagement—for the same reason. Katherine imposed restrictions on the coaching process from the beginning: Tom must not interact with his peers, and the CP was not allowed to interview the peers or anyone else to obtain 360-degree feedback for Tom. The CP was to work only with Tom. The CP requested permission to speak with Katherine's (now retired) predecessor, Tom's former manager and mentor. That request was also denied.

Meanwhile, the CP and Tom were having coaching meetings twice a week. The CP found Tom to be sincere, engaging, able to introspect about his behaviors, and able to express his emotions in an analytical and reflective way. He expressed appreciation for the CP's help in figuring out what to do to save his career and reputation. The CP made a final request of Katherine that she and Tom have a three-way meeting with the CP, figuring that, as a last resort, perhaps a facilitated conversation between them would be helpful (i.e., as "dyadic team building"). That request was also denied. Katherine stated that she didn't have time. The CP was just to work with Tom—no one else—and "get him to get his head on straight." The CP requested a meeting with Katherine to review where they were and to discuss the process. Yet again, the request was denied because she did not have time for such a meeting.

What is to be made of this situation? What could be done and why? Every request for getting needed input to the process was denied. The lawyer continued to take notes every time the CP spoke with Katherine (obviously building a legal case), and Katherine refused to meet with the CP and Tom together. Then she refused to meet again with the CP (she was "too busy").

With Tom's understanding and permission, the CP wrote a letter to Katherine, with a copy to the lawyer who had been present at every meeting between the CP and Katherine and a copy to the TM representative who had recommended the CP to Katherine, withdrawing from the coaching engagement because they had done as much as could be done without input from key stakeholders—or his former manager—to inform the developmental coaching process. The CP also expressed concern that the developmental coaching engagement was disingenuous; Katherine had made no attempt to build a relationship with Tom, the CP and Tom were not allowed to collect key stakeholder feedback to inform their work, Katherine had no time to be involved in Tom's development work, and finally, Katherine didn't have time to meet with the CP again—thus, this letter in lieu of meeting in person or by phone. The CP knew that action would close the door on ever doing business with that executive (and perhaps the company) again. But what was at stake was the welfare of the coaching client and the organization. (Tom had been close with his colleagues who reported to Katherine's position. They had been put in an awkward place as well, having been forbidden to contact Tom.)

Professionally and ethically, the CP felt a responsibility to Tom and did not abandon him when she withdrew from the engagement sponsored by the company. The CP referred Tom to a highly esteemed CP colleague, who did a wonderful job of helping him with "next career move" decisions. That CP reported years later that Tom's career took off again with a different company, and he achieved all that he had wanted—and more.

This case is an example of a professional issue comprising both ethical and moral components. The moral component included the CP's concern about abandoning Tom by disengaging, as well as the issue of continuing to coach Tom and bill the company even though the coaching was disingenuous, and the company (a client also) was not being helped.

Client Readiness for Coaching

Here is another scenario to consider:

A CP, Edward—an I/O psychologist by academic training—was engaged by a top executive to coach a woman (Jean) who had been fast tracked up the management ladder as part of the company's commitment to diversity, equity, and inclusion. She had received a double promotion (two management levels above her position) 9 months prior, and her span of control had more than tripled. As a professional engineer, Jean had excelled in engineering at the company and was rewarded with a management position over engineering. At first, she was thrilled with that promotion. However, she didn't like the administrative aspects of her job and still wanted to be involved in engineering. Her 360-degree feedback reported, among other things, that she was prone to "micromanaging"; kept her door closed except for scheduled meetings, not wanting interruptions; was not developing direct reports; and had frequent emotional outbursts in meetings. Doug, the company's chief operating officer, had reached out to Edward to request a meeting to discuss leadership coaching for Jean, his direct report. He had always been a fan of Jean and had mentored her. In their meeting, Doug disclosed to Edward that his development plan called for the active promotion of women in the organization. Jean was the brightest of his other female leaders and had a national reputation for excellence in engineering—hence, her rapid advancement. However, Doug said she needed help elevating her leadership skills because she was now responsible for a large profit and loss and had a large span of control. In fact, the span of control was too large (actually, for anyone), and Doug said he intended to split that role into two and had initiated a national search for a new leader for the larger of the two roles. In the meantime, he appointed Jean to the combined role. Edward looked forward to working with Jean and was pleased when she reached out to him to schedule a meeting.

In the first meeting, Jean confided to Edward that she struggles with extreme anxiety; had been receiving treatment for it, including in hospital for several months; and still goes to weekly therapy sessions and weekly group meetings. Edward was pleased to hear that Jean was still seeing her therapist, so there was no need to be concerned about the clinical issues because those were being addressed with the therapist. He was extremely conscientious about complying with the ethical standards for psychologists, which included ensuring that one did not practice outside their area of competence (APA Ethics Code, Standard 2.01). The first few coaching meetings went well. Jean was "all in" and prepared for every meeting. The CP found her intuitive, insightful, and self-reflective—which is promising for developing as a leader.

Jean wanted 360-degree feedback from her manager, direct reports, and peers. She had been an interviewee in the 360-degree feedback process of a colleague conducted by Edward 2 years prior and, at that time, had expressed a wish to get that kind of feedback. So, early in the coaching engagement, Edward interviewed her key stakeholders—as always, keeping individuals' comments anonymous. Jean accepted her 360-degree feedback well (actually, she found "no surprises") and was actively involved with Edward in identifying the main key focus areas for development. She then dived in to work on those, fully dedicated to improving her effectiveness as a leader. Following her development plan, she scheduled individual meetings with each of her direct reports, thanked them for their feedback, and summarized her takeaways and what her development goals were, and she asked each person for help in her development journey (e.g., by their giving her feedback). Those individual meetings went so well and everyone was so encouraging and supportive that she told the CP that she wanted to have a leadership team development off site, bringing all her direct reports together for the first time. She threw herself into planning that meeting with the CP, and she showed enthusiasm in looking forward to the event. It was a 2-day meeting. The first day was devoted to getting to know each other better, complete with a couple of well-known individual assessments used in team development. That day went well. Jean was open, showed good humor, and everyone left on a high, looking forward to the next day when they would be working on real-time issues they needed to resolve. That evening, Jean and the CP debriefed that successful first day and did final preparation for the next.

The second day saw a dramatic derailment. It was to be the easier of the 2 days because the focus for team members was not on each other but on real-time issues they needed to work on together. The third issue on the agenda was to review and update the selection criteria for the larger piece of Jean's combined roles. Jean had been looking forward to being relieved of that piece because her role was too large for one person and a source of anxiety. However, as the team began listing the must-have attributes of considered candidates, they included such things as "adjustment—'keeps their cool' in tense situations; active developer of people; and manages conflict well."

Suddenly, Jean panicked. She said she felt personally attacked (because the characteristics they named were not her strong suit). Jean fled the room. Edward called a break and ran after her, but Jean had disappeared. The meeting was over, and everyone returned to their offices. One person was overheard saying, "Yeah, it was too good to be true."

What happened there? To what do you attribute Jean's behavior? What had Edward missed? What would you do now if you were Edward? What would you have done before the blow-up that would have prevented it?

Clinical psychologists reading this know the answers. Nonclinical psychologists may not. Jean had not had sufficient recovery time from her clinical anxiety treatment. Edward had taken comfort in the fact that Jean was still working with her therapist and that she was cheerful and positive about the team development off-site.

Edward reported later that in a peer consultation meeting in which peer colleagues review each other's cases on a confidential basis (with identities of individuals and companies disguised), he had learned (the hard way) that in his firm commitment to the psychologists' ethics code (i.e., adhering to it literally and rigidly by "compartmentalizing" and ignoring the "clinical issues" to make sure he didn't practice outside his areas of competence), he had made a serious mistake. Clinically trained peer colleagues pointed out (the obvious) that the client is one whole person; any clinical issues are with them at all times in varying degrees of expression. Coaching colleagues pointed out that Edward needed to have stepped outside his areas of competence to ensure he was always considering the whole person in coaching. He simply could have asked Jean how her therapy was going and whether she was learning anything there that might have relevance for what they were doing together in coaching, facilitating Jean's making the connections, bringing together her learnings, and paving the way for an important conversation about how she was feeling about her current leader role: what she liked and felt strong in, what was difficult, what kind of things tended to spike her anxiety, and so on. Although Jean and Edward had known that one of the off-site's agenda items was to decide the selection criteria for the role that was to be split off from Jean's current role, Edward had failed to anticipate the emotional impact that might have on Jean at this time, so recently returned from her medical leave and still in therapy.

This was a case of the CP being unaware of what he did not know and an example of misguided assumptions relative to the interpretation of and commitment to APA's Ethics Code. It was also a case of the client not being ready in the first place for taking on the large roles in which she had been placed, and the CP needed to have helped Jean integrate what was going on with her personally, including her therapy, which hopefully would have enabled him to anticipate and avoid situations that would inflame her sensitivities and anxiety. Edward had discussed with Jean's manager at the beginning of the coaching engagement the obvious fact that she wasn't ready for such a big leadership role, but Doug refused to hear it because his feet were being held to the fire to have women in top leader roles, and Jean was the most capable woman in his organization.

There are many more facets to this case, but space limitations preclude addressing them. Suffice it to say that, obviously, this was a selection problem—promoting into two big roles someone whose strong suits were in engineering and technical operations and not in leading and managing and who suffered from extreme anxiety for which she was still being treated. In hindsight, the CP likely would wonder whether he should have discontinued coaching once that became apparent and, if so, what impact that would likely have had on Jean, Doug, and the organization. And as those questions are pondered, the bigger question would certainly surface—whether the CP should have declined the engagement in the first place. This is a case that the reader might want to process in a supervisory consultation with one or more seasoned CPs, preferably one with a clinical background and one with an I/O background.

Fostering a Dependency

Most Level 3 coaching engagements are 6 months to 1 year in duration (Vandaveer et al., 2016, p. 128). However, there are a good number of CPs who maintain client engagements for many years (sometimes 20 or more). Most, perhaps all, of those become Level 4 engagements in which the CP becomes a trusted leadership advisor (Wasylyshyn, 2015). One risk for a CP in such an engagement is that they could become overidentified with the client—and maybe even have a personal stake in client outcomes—to such an extent that they lose their independent perspective and objectivity. In effect, they risk being seen by some as coleading with the client. Evidence of that includes behaviors such as the CP taking great pride in what the client is doing and has achieved (seeming to "take credit" for the organization's results) to such a degree that they are blind to what is happening below their client in the organization, including being in touch with the impact that leader is having on people who report to them. Enjoying being close to the power and thereby having *referent power*—that is, power derived from close association and identification with a person or persons with strong legitimate power (French & Raven, 1959)—they may not be trusted by those lower in the organizational hierarchy. Having become closely identified with their primary client, they may express exhilaration at successes that "we [the client and CP] achieved." Although they may remain engaged with that client for years, they—like their client—can get out of touch with what is happening below and not realize that they are not trusted by many in the organization.

Engaging in regular periodic peer consultations (or coach supervision, as it is sometimes referred to) is advisable, no matter how advanced the CP's expertise, to review cases (confidentially and keeping the client's anonymity) and help keep oneself sharp and objective to be of greatest value to the client.

Mandated Coaching

Most executive and leader development coaching is provided for individuals who are already in a leadership position and want to develop their leadership skills further or who are considered to have "high potential" for becoming an effective leader. Executive and leadership coaching is considered an investment in the company's leadership talent, anticipating a good return in the form of higher productivity and a healthier organizational climate, which also help to elicit individuals' best performance. Occasionally, however, a CP will be called to coach an individual whose performance or behavior is not meeting expectations and whose manager has demanded they get coaching—that is, the person has been sent to coaching (like to the principal's office). Some CPs specialize in working with poor performers; however, many or most CPs are engaged to help those with leadership and/or executive potential or who are already in significant leader roles get to the "top of their game."

When a CP gets a call about coaching a poor performer, it will be important to understand the situation before signing on. For example, in addition to learning about the problematic behaviors of the individual, the CP needs to know what has been done already that hasn't been successful enough, including especially what the manager has done and what role the manager intends to take in the individual's developmental coaching work. Frankly, there are too many cases of a manager not doing their job in dealing effectively with substandard performance. In our experience, we have encountered several managers who offload responsibility for dealing with poor performance to a coach because they prefer not to deal with it. (Sometimes it's the manager who needs coaching in how to inspire the best performance, confront substandard performance directly—in a supportive way—and work with the individual, setting specific improvement goals with manager coaching and follow-up.) Thus, when called to coach a substandard performer, the first step is to discuss the situation and needs with the manager, including learning what has been done to try to correct the observed problems. If it appears to the CP that the manager has written the person off and is not working to help them improve, the CP needs to know what the individual's prospects are. Does the manager intend to fire them? Is the manager avoiding their responsibility to provide effective feedback and coaching to those who report to them?

The CP always needs to be on the lookout for the possibility of a disingenuous motive on the manager's part, such as intending to fire the individual but wanting to be able to document that "I even provided him with a coach." That is a big red flag. If the manager seems sincere, with the intent of helping the individual "re-rail," the next step is to meet with the individual. If the individual has a negative attitude about "being sent to coaching," the CP can seek to learn their perspectives and feelings about their performance and the coaching process. If there is a positive response to the prospect of working in confidence with the CP, it may be worth engaging and seeing if the CP can indeed help. However, if what the CP senses from any of these steps is that either the manager has already written off the potential client and this process is only perfunctory for the purpose of checking a box, or if the individual is clearly not ready for coaching, the CP needs to walk away because the prospects for a good outcome are dim.

In the next sections, we raise some different professional issues that CPs need to consider: professional licensure, self-care, coaching caveats, and related issues.

Licensure

Licensing laws for psychologists in the United States or Canada are set by each state or province, and they differ from one to another. It is the responsibility of each CP to know what the licensing law and licensing board rules and regulations are in their state. In some states, psychologists who do only organizational consulting or executive coaching are exempt from licensure. A few states do not license psychologists who are not health service providers (e.g., clinical, counseling, or school psychologists). Some states require licensure if a person with an advanced degree in psychology does any kind of testing or assessment and makes or recommends decisions about people based on the results or if their practice includes other things specified in the licensing act in that state.

Psychologists who are licensed in their state of residence and want to practice across state lines need to be familiar with the licensing law in each state in which they want to practice. Some states grant reciprocity with one's home state, some states allow a certain number of days practicing in their state without requiring a license, and other states have different provisions. For information on requirements, in addition to checking out one's own state's requirements, a great deal of useful information can be found on the website of the Association of State and Provincial Psychology Boards: https://www.asppb.net/page/psybook. Whether or not one becomes licensed as a psychologist, it is highly recommended that all CPs arrange to have peer consultation (some refer to it as *peer supervision*) throughout their professional practice lives.

Professional Development and Self-Care

As the primary instrument in facilitating another person's learning and development, the CP must keep themself in top condition—mentally, physically, and emotionally. A few examples follow:

- Stay abreast of the evolving science relative to coaching psychology and leadership and breakthroughs in professional practice that elevate the effectiveness of the CP and coaching.

- Engage in periodic, regular peer consultation that includes case review and analysis; identify a trusted colleague who is willing to consult on just-in-time case questions or quandaries.

- Prepare well for each coaching meeting; establish a discipline about preparing for coaching meetings and consider including mindful practice as part of that.

- Take continuing education classes and workshops (whether or not it is required to maintain a license!). The learning is invaluable, and it is a good way to keep abreast of the science and ensure that (a) ethical issues and (b) culture-related topics, including diversity, equity, and inclusion, are part of every year's learnings and continuing education.

- Present at professional conferences for which program proposals are peer reviewed and accepted or rejected and/or publish in peer-reviewed journals (helping to ensure one contributes to and keeps up with the science).

- Monitor workload and stress levels; balance pursuit of income with the need to have time to recharge and reflect; consider referring coaching cases to trusted coaching colleagues rather than squeezing every billable minute into the workweek.

- Keep mind, body, and spirit healthy, however one chooses to do that. Some examples are exercising regularly, eating properly, practicing yoga and meditation, engaging in whatever self-expressive activity nourishes one's spirit (e.g., music, dance, sport, being in nature), and getting adequate sleep.

Coaching Caveats and Considerations About Accepting a Coaching Engagement

CPs, like all professionals, need to think carefully about the likelihood of success before accepting an engagement. Professionals must ask themselves, "Does the client's request align with my experience and expertise?" "Have I explored any special adjustments or requests that the client has made?" "How ready is the organization to support individuals' growth and development?" Even when client requests seem familiar and typical, true professionals explore wider questions, such as those in the previous section, before accepting a project. It is also every professional's responsibility to commit to a timeline for completion that is feasible given other commitments.

Coaching assignments are likely to be less standardized than other types of consulting projects. Even in the early precontracting conversations between coach and sponsors, the coach needs to explore various factors that can either positively or negatively affect coaching outcomes. The CP is responsible for raising questions that the sponsoring organization may not have thought about but that can significantly impact the results. Although this is primarily a practice issue (i.e., the coach properly scoping out the work to inform contracting and communicating transparent and acceptable expectations), it is also an ethics issue in avoiding overcommitment and underdelivery, even unknowingly. A key part of being a CP is critically evaluating client requests, even familiar ones; discussing concerns; and possibly resolving them before beginning the engagement. To the extent that problematic information is revealed, coaches, as with any professional, need to include pertinent considerations in the contracting process or decline the engagement entirely. Competence and transparency require that projects be declined when significant doubts about viability exist.

This is especially true of coaching because outcomes can be difficult to describe a priori, and human behavior is so variable and often unique. To clarify the types of variables coaches should explore before taking on an assignment, I (MF) have published two short articles (see Chapter 3), anchored in my case experience, highlighting factors that may contribute to coaching derailment or not completely delivering on expectations (Frisch, 2005a, 2005b). Some of these are difficult to explore fully before coaching begins, but data on all of them are obtainable if the coach skillfully questions organizational sponsors. Not doing so and then having coaching yield disappointing results is certainly a practice gap, but it also touches on a lack of professional rigor. The following rubric is intended as a practical guard against that and an encouragement to coaches to contract knowledgeably and step away from engagements encumbered by too many caveats or unknowns.

In examining coaching cases over a 5-year period while leading a regional coaching practice for a consulting firm, I found that two main domains were contributing to disappointing coaching outcomes: (a) organizational context and (b) characteristics of the coaching client (Frisch, 2005a, 2005b). Going further, I identified five specific factors, or caveats, under each domain. These define in practical terms the areas the coach can explore in precoaching stages, building the results into informed contracting or even delaying or declining a coaching engagement. The first factor in each domain is defined as a *go/no-go* decision, while the other four factors in each domain are variables that can range more widely.

Organizational Context Caveats

Equivocal Organizational Commitment (Go/No-Go Toggle). Equivocal organizational commitment is indicated by sponsors who express uncertainty about the value, or likely success, of investing in the client's development and may even be equivocal about retaining the client in the organization. Coaching should not begin until the sponsoring organization can assure the coach of developmental support for the client during and after the coaching engagement.

Organization Upheaval. The organization can be in significant flux for many reasons, such as a merger, acquisition, divestiture, downsizing, outsourcing, and hiring a new CEO. Such upheaval can be a significant distraction to coaching, especially if layoffs are occurring. However, coaching can be helpful for executives leading or experiencing a lot of change (provided, of course, that the CP's experience and expertise includes organizational change).

Sponsor–Client Relationship. All experienced CPs understand that a key influence on a client's behavior, for better or worse, is the client's direct manager. That manager should support the client's development and commit to furthering the implementation of the development plan produced in most coaching engagements. If the client's relationship with the manager is conflicted, there is mistrust, or the manager is absent because of location or work demands, a key pillar for development could be weak, and/or that relationship may be a key focus area for coaching work.

Coaching as Part of a Mandated Program. When coaching is tied to a broader organizational program, such as leadership training or a feedback process, the success of the coaching is, to varying extents, tied to the effectiveness of that larger program. To the extent that the client is ready for the program and the program is delivered well, the coaching component is typically well supported. To the extent that executives are mandated to attend, with participants simply checking the box, or if there are other issues with delivery, the effectiveness of coaching may suffer too.

Note that all these caveats, except perhaps the first, are not necessarily showstoppers. However, CPs who are beginning coaching are advised to make themselves knowledgeable about the situation and proceed only if they know they have the skills to make a positive difference.

Potential Caveats Relative to the Coaching Client

Significant Personal or Familial Problems, Upheaval, or Upset in the Client's Life (Go/No-Go Toggle). Although coaching may be viewed as an organization's gift to an individual, it also involves a significant commitment of time and energy on the part of the client. Clients who are stressed by personal or family challenges (e.g., illness, grief, family upheaval, drug abuse) are less likely to have the emotional and cognitive stamina to use and benefit from coaching. When a client shares such concerns with coaches early on or even before coaching begins, the CP, using fine-tuned dialogic skills, should engage in dialogue and, together with the client, decide whether coaching should be delayed. If CP and client decide that it would be best to delay coaching until things settle down, the CP support the client's request to their sponsors that coaching be delayed. CPs can support those requests at the same time as containing confidential information about the client.

Risk Tolerance: The Willingness to Try New Approaches and Tolerate Some Discomfort, Awkwardness, and Vulnerability; Self-Efficacy. Coaching often requires that people try new approaches, which requires a certain level of tolerance to exposure and the risk that comes with both experimentation and confidence about outcomes. Clients whose confidence or sense of self-efficacy needs significant strengthening may not be ready for a coaching process that requires trying new behaviors right away.

In such cases, the focus of coaching work may, therefore, initially be working on those limiting factors. One can usually assume that the company invests in people they consider valuable to the organization; therefore, it is important that the CP "take the client where they are" and help them build these necessary intrapersonal skills. In cases of severe incapacitating discomfort or low self-esteem, clients may need clinical psychological therapy before—or along with—coaching to get the most out of the leadership development coaching process. This is a potential caveat: CPs who are new to coaching and/or do not have significant experience in helping clients overcome these issues are advised to refer the client to a seasoned CP who is highly skilled in these areas.

Emotional Resilience: The Ability to Consider Feedback, Depersonalize Setbacks, and Stay Motivated to Own Change. Emotional resilience focuses on inner reactions to outer events, such as feedback from others. It involves the ability to resist defensiveness and translate feedback into behavioral change. An implicit goal of all coaching is to normalize seeking feedback and becoming able to consider—and eventually value—it. Feedback about the gap between a leader's intentions and their impact on others can be emotionally challenging to absorb and use in planning the best way to shrink that gap. Coaching clients whose first inclination is to become angry in response to constructive or negative feedback will be unable to use it to improve; therefore, effective work on that will need to happen first.

Psychological Curiosity and Insight. If the client is interested in understanding why people do what they do and what antecedents generally precede particular behaviors, that will likely be helpful for positive change in coaching. Self-insight, especially about the connection between feelings and behavior, supports changes clients are trying to make. It is invaluable in deepening dialogue about interpersonal situations the client faces. Clients lacking interest in understanding themselves or others are likely to make slower progress in their change efforts. A caveat to this potential caveat is that individuals in organizations are always interested in themselves and their success, however they define it. The skilled CP will find a way to "hook into" those basic motivational drivers and can often spark the client's interest in understanding "why" as they pursue the "what" and "how" of achieving their aspirations.

The Classic Motivation to Change. Motivation to change is routinely discussed before most coaching assignments: How motivated is the client to change? These conversations sometimes touch on the aforementioned variables, but a useful conceptualization of motivation is provided by the transtheoretical model of change (DiClemente & Prochaska, 1998). This model clearly defines the stages leading to change efforts, from precontemplation (no awareness of the possible need to change) to full involvement in the change process. Clients in the early stages of this model are likely to make slower progress in coaching. The impact of organizational rewards may also play into this variable. The greater the extent to which the client's development can be tied, even indirectly, to their career aspirations, the stronger their motivation to grow and change is likely to be (Boyatzis & Jack, 2018; Boyatzis et al., 2019).

Summary

Rigorous contracting of a possible coaching engagement should touch on most, if not all, of these caveats. Although the first variable in each domain involves a go/no-go decision, all the others are scalable. Furthermore, in our experience, they are also cumulative. For example, if an organization is unstable and the client is rejecting feedback or risk averse, these variables may combine to compromise coaching outcomes further. CPs need to help sponsoring organizations explore these variables and, if possible, find ways of mitigating them, such as providing more time for coaching, more checkpoints, or other specific adjustments. However, if the coach's professional judgment indicates there are significant caveats active and the likelihood of success is low, the coaching engagement can be declined, with an explanation based on the caveats (Welsh et al., 2015).

CONCLUSION

Ethics and professionalism are inextricably linked. In fact, ethical guidelines operationalize some essential aspects of professionalism. From early contracting to meetings with clients to assessment feedback to fostering developmental discussions between client and sponsors, a coach's professional judgment must always be sound. Familiarity between organizational sponsors and coaches is always helpful, but every client presents new considerations. Professionals avoid assumptions and generalizations in favor of frank exploration of the upside and downside of new engagements. In leadership coaching, as in medicine, an ounce of prevention is worth a pound of cure. In this chapter, we have intended to raise awareness of ethical and professional issues and help arm the CP with knowledge and resources to help ensure their professional judgment is always at a level where ethical risks are minimized.

Epilogue

E xecutive coaching is a relatively new area of professional practice in psychology, but it has grown rapidly and has thousands of skilled practitioners around the globe. Although the argument might be made that psychologists originated one-to-one helping in the work context, the field of executive coaching has many more nonpsychologist providers. We believe there is a huge opportunity for more psychologists to experience this gratifying and sustaining professional practice that contributes to organizations' effectiveness and psychologically healthier workplaces. Who better than psychologists to partner with organizational clients to foster professional growth; leadership; organizational, individual, and team performance, including complex organization transformation and culture change; and/or individuals' career aspirations? Although significant formal training and some years of professional practice with feedback and mentoring and/or peer consultation are required to be skilled in extrapolating the knowledge from psychological science and learnings from professional practice into one's professional practice of executive coaching, for those psychologists who are interested in the world of work, it is well worth the developmental effort to become a coaching psychologist (CP).

No one knows for sure what the future will bring. We wrote this book during the worst pandemic in a century and as other societal crises came into sharper focus. Coaching has continued to grow even in this challenging period. The Institute of Coaching (2021) argued that all these events have radically altered what it means to be an effective leader. Their key point was that leaders need to shift toward an emphasis on humanity and connectedness if they and their organizations are to succeed. We expect that leadership coaching will continue, and maybe even accelerate, leadership change in that direction; therefore, coaching as an intervention and coaching as a professional service will be in even stronger demand. We see these trends extrapolating into more academic programs on leadership coaching in the United States, as well as growth in all types of coaching and coaches who are both internal and external to the organizations they serve.

Our aim with this modest book is to help make the path to becoming a leadership CP a bit clearer and easier. We hope it both inspires increased interest in the field and informs those psychologists who have already decided to include it in their professional work. As we know from psychological science, and as we observe in our coaching clients, change begins with intention and is facilitated in large part by partnering with knowledgeable guides. We offer this book in the spirit of partnership with you, the reader, on your path to becoming a fully prepared CP.

References

Albizu, E., Rekalde, I., Landeta, J., & Fernández-Ferrín, P. (2019). Analysis of executive coaching effectiveness: A study from the coachee perspective. *Cuadernos de Gestión, 19*(2), 33–52. https://doi.org/10.5295/cdg.170876ea

American Educational Research Association, American Psychological Association, & National Council on Measurement in Education. (2014). *Standards for educational and psychological testing* (6th ed.). https://www.testingstandards.net/open-access-files.html

American Psychological Association. (2017). *Ethical principles of psychologists and code of conduct* (2002, Amended June 1, 2010, and January 1, 2017). https://www.apa.org/ethics/code/index.aspx

Anderson, M. C. (2011). Evaluating the ROI of coaching: Telling a story not just producing a number. In G. Hernez-Broome & L. A. Boyce (Eds.), *Advancing executive coaching: Setting the course for successful leadership coaching* (pp. 351–368). Wiley.

Argyris, C., & Schön, D. A. (1974). *Theory in practice: Increasing professional effectiveness*. Jossey-Bass.

Athanasopoulou, A., & Dopson, S. (2018). A systematic review of coaching outcomes: Is it the journey or the destination that matters the most? *The Leadership Quarterly, 29*(1), 70–88. https://doi.org/10.1016/j.leaqua.2017.11.004

Axelrod, S. D. (2005). Executive growth along the adult development curve. *Consulting Psychology Journal, 57*(2), 118–125. https://doi.org/10.1037/1065-9293.57.2.118

Axelrod, W. (2019). *10 steps to successful mentoring*. Association for Talent Development.

Bachkirova, T. (2016). The self of the coach: Conceptualization, issues, and opportunities for practitioner development. *Consulting Psychology Journal, 68*(2), 143–156. https://doi.org/10.1037/cpb0000055

Baron, L., & Morin, L. (2010). The impact of executive coaching on self-efficacy related to management soft-skills. *Leadership and Organization Development Journal, 31*(1), 18–38. https://doi.org/10.1108/01437731011010362

Behrendt, P., Muhlberger, C., Goritz, A. S., & Jonas, E. (2021). Relationship, purpose, and change—An integrative model of coach behavior. *Consulting Psychology Journal, 73*(2), 103–121. https://doi.org/10.1037/cpb0000197

Boyatzis, R. E., & Jack, A. I. (2018). The neuroscience of coaching. *Consulting Psychology Journal, 70*(1), 11–27. https://doi.org/10.1037/cpb0000095

Boyatzis, R. E., & McKee, A. (2005). *Resonant leadership: Renewing yourself and connecting with others through mindfulness, hope, and compassion.* Harvard Business School Press.

Boyatzis, R., Smith, M., & Van Oosten, E. (2019). *Helping people change: Coaching with compassion for lifelong learning and growth.* Harvard Business Review Press.

Carroll, M. (2008). Coaching psychology supervision. In S. Palmer & A. Whybrow (Eds.), *Handbook of coaching psychology* (pp. 431–448). Routledge.

Cavanagh, M., Grant, A., & Kemp, T. (2005). *Evidence-based coaching: Volume 1. Theory, research and practice from the behavioural sciences.* Australian Academic Press.

Clay, R. A. (2017). Taking a hard look: Self-assessment tools and strategies can help practitioners ensure they are practicing competently. *Monitor on Psychology, 48*(5), 46–51. https://www.apa.org/monitor/2017/05/hard-look

The Conference Board. (2018). *Global executive coaching survey report.* https://www.conference-board.org/topics/executive-coaching/global-executive-coaching-survey-2018-report

Coultas, C. W., Bedwell, W. L., Burke, C., & Salas, E. (2011). Values sensitive coaching: The DELTA approach to coaching culturally diverse executives. *Consulting Psychology Journal, 63*(3), 149–161. https://doi.org/10.1037/a0025603

Courtney, C. L., & Vandaveer, V. V. (2013, February 10). *Role of coach: Self as instrument in the executive development process* [Workshop]. Annual Mid-Winter Conference of the Society of Consulting Psychology, APA Division 13, Atlanta, GA, United States.

Cox, E., Bachkirova, T., & Clutterbuck, D. (2014). *The complete handbook of coaching psychology* (2nd ed.). SAGE.

De Cremer, D., van Dick, R., & Murnighan, K. (Eds.). (2012). *Social psychology and organizations.* Routledge Taylor & Francis.

de Haan, E. (2008). *Relational coaching: Journeys toward mastering one-to-one learning*. Wiley.

de Haan, E., Duckworth, A., Birch, D., & Jones, C. (2013). Executive coaching outcome research: The contribution of common factors such as relationship, personality match, and self-efficacy. *Consulting Psychology Journal, 65*(1), 40–57. https://doi.org/10.1037/a0031635

de Haan, E., Grant, A. M., Burger, Y., & Eriksson, P.-O. (2016). A large-scale study of executive and workplace coaching: The relative contributions of relationship, personality match, and self-efficacy. *Consulting Psychology Journal, 68*(3), 189–207. https://doi.org/10.1037/cpb0000058

de Haan, E., Gray, D. E., & Bonneywell, S. (2019). Executive coaching outcome research in a field setting: A near-randomized controlled trial study in a global healthcare corporation. *Academy of Management Learning & Education, 18*(4), 581–605. https://doi.org/10.5465/amle.2018.0158

de Haan, E., Molyn, J., & Nilsson, V. O. (2020). New findings on the effectiveness of the coaching relationship: Time to think differently about active ingredients? *Consulting Psychology Journal, 72*(3), 155–167. https://doi.org/10.1037/cpb0000175

De Meuse, K. P., Dai, G., & Lee, R. J. (2009). Evaluating the effectiveness of executive coaching: Beyond ROI? *Coaching, 2*(2), 117–134. https://doi.org/10.1080/17521880902882413

Dewey, J. (1938). *Education and experience*. Simon & Schuster.

DiClemente, C. C., & Prochaska, J. O. (1998). Toward a comprehensive, transtheoretical model of change: Stages of change and addictive behaviors. In W. R. Miller & N. Heather (Eds.), *Treating addictive behaviors* (2nd ed., pp. 3–24). Plenum Press. https://doi.org/10.1007/978-1-4899-1934-2_1

Dixit, P., & Dixit, P. (2018). Applications of neuroscience in coaching. *NHRD Network Journal, 11*(4), 56–62. https://doi.org/10.1177/2631454118806138

Drake, D. B. (2009). Using attachment theory in coaching leaders: The search for a coherent narrative. *International Coaching Psychology Review, 4*(1), 49–58.

Ducharme, M. J. (2004). The cognitive-behavioral approach to executive coaching. *Consulting Psychology Journal, 56*(4), 214–224. https://doi.org/10.1037/1065-9293.56.4.214

Ely, K., & Zaccaro, S. (2011). Evaluating the effectiveness of coaching: A focus on stakeholders, criteria, and data collection methods. In G. Hernez-Broome & L. A. Boyce (Eds.), *Advancing executive coaching: Setting the course for successful leadership coaching* (pp. 319–350). Wiley.

Ernest, P. (1991). *The philosophy of mathematics education: Studies in mathematics education*. Falmer.

Feltham, C., & Palmer, S. (2015). An introduction to counselling and psycho-therapy. In S. Palmer (Ed.), *The beginner's guide to counselling & psychotherapy* (pp. 4–19). SAGE. https://doi.org/10.4135/9781473918061.n2

Flaherty, J. (2010). *Coaching: Evoking excellence in others* (3rd ed.). Routledge. https://doi.org/10.4324/9780080964294

Fosnot, C. T. (1996). Constructivism: A psychological theory of learning. In C. Fosnot (Ed.), *Constructivism: Theory, perspectives, and practice* (pp. 8–33). Teachers College Press.

Fosnot, C. T., & Perry, R. S. (2005). Constructivism: A psychological theory of learning. In C. Fosnot (Ed.), *Constructivism: Theory, perspectives, and practice* (2nd ed., pp. 8–33). Teachers College Press.

French, J. R. P., & Raven, B. (1959). The bases of social power. In D. Cartwright (Ed.), *Studies in social power* (pp. 150–167). University of Michigan Institute for Social Research. http://www.communicationcache.com/uploads/1/0/8/8/10887248/the_bases_of_social_power_-_chapter_20_-_1959.pdf

Frisch, M. H. (2001). The emerging role of the internal coach. *Consulting Psychology Journal, 53*(4), 240–250. https://doi.org/10.1037/1061-4087.53.4.240

Frisch, M. H. (2005a). Coaching caveats: Part 1: Organizational context. *Human Resource Planning, 28*(2), 13–15. https://go.gale.com/ps/anonymous?id=GALE%7CA134575810&sid=googleScholar&v=2.1&it=r&linkaccess=abs&issn=01998986&p=AONE&sw=w

Frisch, M. H. (2005b). Coaching caveats: Part 2: Characteristics of the coachee. *Human Resource Planning, 28*(3), 14–16. https://go.gale.com/ps/anonymous?id=GALE%7CA138142109&sid=googleScholar&v=2.1&it=r&linkaccess=abs&issn=01998986&p=AONE&sw=w

Frisch, M. H. (2008). *Use of self in executive coaching* [Unpublished monograph].

Frisch, M. H. (2019). *Coaching psychology: Consulting psychology interventions at the level of the individual* [Unpublished monograph].

Frisch, M. H., Lee, R. J., Metzger, K., Robinson, J., & Rosemarin, J. (2012). *Becoming an exceptional executive coach: Use your knowledge, experience, and intuition to help leaders excel.* AMACOM.

Gallwey, W. T. (1997). *The inner game of tennis: The classic guide to the mental side of peak performance.* Random House.

Garman, A. N. (2002). Assessing candidates for leadership positions. In R. Lowman (Ed.), *Handbook of consulting psychology* (pp. 185–211). Wiley.

Gebhardt, J. A. (2016). Quagmires for clinical psychology and executive coaching? Ethical considerations and practice challenges. *American Psychologist, 71*(3), 216–235. https://doi.org/10.1037/a0039806

Grant, A. (2013). The efficacy of coaching. In J. Passmore, D. Peterson, & T. Freire (Eds.), *The Wiley-Blackwell handbook of the psychology of coaching and mentoring* (pp. 15–39). Wiley-Blackwell.

Grant, A., & Cavanagh, M. (2007). Evidence-based coaching: Flourishing or languishing? *Australian Psychologist, 42*(4), 239–254. https://doi.org/10.1080/00050060701648175

Grant, A., Passmore, J., Cavanagh, M., & Parker, H. (2010). The state of play in coaching today: A comprehensive review of the field. In G. P. Hodgkinson & J. K. Ford (Eds.), *International review of industrial and organizational psychology: Vol. 25. International review of industrial and organizational psychology 2010* (pp. 125–167). Wiley-Blackwell. https://doi.org/10.1002/9780470661628.ch4

Graßmann, C., Schölmerich, F., & Schermuly, C. C. (2020). The relationship between working alliance and client outcomes in coaching: A meta-analysis. *Human Relations, 73*(1), 35–58. https://doi.org/10.1177/0018726718819725

Gregory, J. B., & Levy, P. E. (2015). *Using feedback in organizational consulting.* American Psychological Association. https://doi.org/10.1037/14619-000

Grover, S., & Furnham, A. (2016). Coaching as a developmental intervention in organisations: A systematic review of its effectiveness and the mechanisms underlying it. *PLOS ONE, 11*, e0159137. https://doi.org/10.1371/journal.pone.0159137

Gullette, E. C. D., Fennig, J., Reynolds, T., Humphrey, C., Kinser, M., & Doverspike, D. (2019). Guidelines for Education and Training at the Doctoral and Postdoctoral Levels in Consulting Psychology/Organizational Consulting Psychology: Executive summary of the 2017 revision. *American Psychologist, 74*(5), 608–614. https://doi.org/10.1037/amp0000462

Hackman, J. R. (2002). *Leading teams: Setting the stage for great performances.* Harvard Business School Press.

Hart, V., Blattner, J., & Leipsic, S. (2001). Coaching versus therapy: A perspective. *Consulting Psychology Journal, 53*(4), 229–237. https://doi.org/10.1037/1061-4087.53.4.229

Hawkins, P. (2012). *Creating a coaching culture.* Open University Press, McGraw Hill.

Hawkins, P. (2014). Coaching supervision. In E. Cox, T. Bachkirova, & D. Clutterbuck (Eds.), *The complete handbook of coaching psychology* (2nd ed., pp. 391–404). SAGE.

Healey, M. L., & Grossman, M. (2018). Cognitive and affective perspective-taking: Evidence for shared and dissociable anatomical substrates. *Frontiers in Neurology, 9*, 491. https://doi.org/10.3389/fneur.2018.00491

Hernez-Broome, G., & Boyce, L. A. (Eds.). (2011). *Advancing executive coaching: Setting the course for successful leadership coaching.* Jossey-Bass.

Hofstede, G. H. (2001). *Culture's consequences: Comparing values, behaviors, institutions, and organizations across nations* (2nd ed.). SAGE.

House, R. J., Hanges, P. J., Javidan, M., Dorfman, P. W., & Gupta, V. (2004). *Culture, leadership, and organizations: The GLOBE study of 62 societies.* SAGE.

Institute of Coaching. (2021). *Leading with humanity: The future of leadership and coaching.* https://instituteofcoaching.org/ioc-report-leading-with-humanity-the-future-of-leadership-coaching

Isaacs, W. (1999). *Dialogue: The art of thinking together.* Crown Archetype.

Jeanneret, P., & Silzer, R. (1998). *Individual psychological assessment: Predicting behavior in organizational settings.* Pfeiffer.

Jones, R. J., Woods, S. A., & Guillaume, Y. R. F. (2016). The effectiveness of workplace coaching: A meta-analysis of learning and performance outcomes from coaching. *Journal of Occupational and Organizational Psychology, 89*(2), 249–277. https://doi.org/10.1111/joop.12119

Kaney, T. (2017). Transitioning into the role of trusted leadership advisor. *Consulting Psychology Journal, 69*(1), 29–31. https://doi.org/10.1037/cpb0000080

Katz, D., & Kahn, R. L. (1978). *The social psychology of organizations.* Wiley.

Kauffman, C., & Hodgetts, W. H. (2016). Model agility: Coaching effectiveness and four perspectives on a case study. *Consulting Psychology Journal, 68*(2), 157–176. https://doi.org/10.1037/cpb0000062

Kilburg, R. R. (2000). *Executive coaching: Developing managerial wisdom in a world of chaos.* American Psychological Association. https://doi.org/10.1037/10355-000

Kilburg, R. R. (2016). The development of human expertise: Toward a model for the 21st century practice of coaching, consulting, and general applied psychology. *Consulting Psychology Journal, 68*(2), 177–187. https://doi.org/10.1037/cpb0000054

Kilburg, R. R., & Diedrich, R. C. (Eds.). (2007). *The wisdom of coaching: Essential papers in consulting psychology for a world of change.* American Psychological Association. https://doi.org/10.1037/11570-000

Kirkpatrick, D. L. (1976). Evaluation of training. In R. I. Craig (Ed.), *Training and development handbook: A guide in human resource development* (2nd ed., pp. 1–27). McGraw-Hill.

Kirkpatrick, D. L. (1994). *Evaluating training programs: The four levels.* Berrett-Koehler.

Kolb, D. (2015). *Experiential learning: Experience as the source of learning and development* (2nd ed.). Pearson Education.

Kolb, D., & Boyatzis, R. (2001). Experiential learning theory: Previous research and new directions. In R. J. Sternberg & L. F. Zhang (Eds.), *Perspectives on thinking, learning, and cognitive styles* (pp. 227–247). Erlbaum.

Lane, D., & Corrie, S. (2009). Does coaching psychology need the concept of formulation? *International Coaching Psychology Review, 4*(2), 195–208. https://doi.org/10.1002/9781119656913.ch6

Laske, O. (2007). Contributions of evidence-based developmental coaching to coaching psychology and practice. *International Coaching Psychology Review, 2*(2), 202–212. https://psycnet.apa.org/record/2007-19806-009

Lee, R. J. (2013). The role of contracting in coaching: Balancing individual client and organizational issues. In J. Passmore, D. Peterson, & T. Freire (Eds.), *The Wiley-Blackwell handbook of the psychology of coaching and mentoring* (pp. 40–57). Wiley-Blackwell.

Lee, R. J., & Frisch, M. H. (2011). Learning to coach leaders. In G. Hernez-Broome & L. A. Boyce (Eds.), *Advancing executive coaching: Setting the course for successful leadership coaching* (pp. 47–81). Jossey-Bass.

Lee, R. J., & Frisch, M. H. (2015). Legacy reflections: Ten lessons about becoming an executive coach. *Consulting Psychology Journal, 67*(1), 3–16. https://doi.org/10.1037/cpb0000033

Lewin, K. (1951). *Field theory in social sciences.* Harper & Row.

Lowman, R. L. (1998). Consulting to organizations as if the individual mattered. *Consulting Psychology Journal, 50*(1), 17–24. https://doi.org/10.1037/1061-4087.50.1.17

Lowman, R. L. (Ed.). (2002). *Handbook of organizational consulting psychology.* Jossey-Bass.

Lowman, R. L. (2007). Coaching and consulting in multicultural contexts: Integrating themes and issues. *Consulting Psychology Journal, 59*(4), 296–303. https://doi.org/10.1037/1065-9293.59.4.296

Lowman, R. L. (2016a). *An introduction to consulting psychology: Working with individuals, groups, and organizations.* American Psychological Association. https://doi.org/10.1037/14853-000

Lowman, R. L. (2016b). *The psychologist as managerial coach.* Oxford University Press. https://doi.org/10.1093/oxfordhb/9780199935291.013.27

Lowman, R. L. (2021). *Career assessment: Integrating interests, abilities, and personality.* American Psychological Association. https://doi.org/10.1037/0000254-000

Lowman, R. L., & Cooper, S. E. (2018). *The ethical practice of consulting psychology.* American Psychological Association. https://doi.org/10.1037/0000058-000

Manuso, J. S. J. (Ed.). (1983). *Occupational clinical psychology.* Praeger.

Maslow, A. H. (1943). A theory of human motivation. *Psychological Review, 50*(4), 370–396. https://doi.org/10.1037/h0054346

McCauley, C., Damiano, P., Graham, P., & Vandaveer, V. (2021, April 15–17). *Coaching executive teams: An I-O perspective* [Panel discussion]. Annual Conference of the Society of Industrial-Organizational Psychology (virtual).

McKenna, D. D., & Davis, S. L. (2009). Hidden in plain sight: The active ingredients of executive coaching. *Perspectives on Industrial and Organizational Psychology, 2*(3), 244–260. https://doi.org/10.1111/j.1754-9434.2009.01143.x

Miller, W. R., & Rollnick, S. (2002). *Motivational interviewing: Preparing people for change* (2nd ed.). Guilford Press.

Moen, F., & Skaalvik, E. (2009). The effect from executive coaching on performance psychology. *International Journal of Evidence Based Coaching and Mentoring, 7*(2), 31–49. https://psycnet.apa.org/record/2010-18728-003

Morrish, J. (2020, August 20). Where the word "mentoring" comes from. *Management Today*. https://www.managementtoday.co.uk/word-mentoring-comes/food-for-thought/article/1397303

Nowack, K., & Mashihi, S. (2012). Evidence-based answers to 15 questions about leveraging 360-degree feedback. *Consulting Psychology Journal, 64*(3), 157–182. https://doi.org/10.1037/a0030011

O'Neil, M. (2000). *Executive coaching with backbone and heart*. Wiley.

Osatuke, K., Yanovsky, B., & Ramsel, D. (2017). Executive coaching: New framework for evaluation. *Consulting Psychology Journal, 69*(3), 172–186. https://doi.org/10.1037/cpb0000073

Page, N., & de Haan, E. (2014). Does executive coaching work? *The Psychologist, 27*(8), 582–587. https://thepsychologist.bps.org.uk/volume-27/edition-8/does-executive-coaching-work

Palmer, S., & Whybrow, A. (Eds.). (2008). *Handbook of coaching psychology*. Routledge.

Passmore, J. (2007). An integrative model for executive coaching. *Consulting Psychology Journal, 59*(1), 68–78. https://doi.org/10.1037/1065-9293.59.1.68

Passmore, J. (Ed.). (2013). *Diversity in coaching: Working with gender, culture, race and age*. Kogan Page.

Passmore, J., Peterson, D. B., & Freire, T. (2013). *The Wiley-Blackwell handbook of the psychology of coaching and mentoring*. Wiley.

Peltier, B. (2010). *The psychology of executive coaching: Theory and application* (2nd ed.). Routledge. https://doi.org/10.4324/9780203886106

Peterson, D. B. (1993). Skill learning and behavior change in an individually tailored management coaching and training program [Doctoral dissertation]. *Dissertation Abstracts International: B. The Sciences and Engineering, 54*, 1707–1708.

Peterson, D. B. (2007). Executive coaching in a cross-cultural context. *Consulting Psychology Journal, 59*(4), 261–271. https://doi.org/10.1037/1065-9293.59.4.261

Peterson, D. (2010). Executive coaching: A critical review and recommendations for advancing the practice. In S. Zedeck (Ed.), *APA handbook of industrial and organizational psychology: Vol. 2. Selecting and developing members of the organization* (pp. 527–566). American Psychological Association.

Pfeffer, J. (2010). *Power*. HarperCollins.

Piaget, J. (1952). *The origins of intelligence in children*. International University Press. https://doi.org/10.1037/11494-000

Piaget, J. (1968). *Structuralism*. Harper Torchbooks.

Prokopeak, M. (2018, March 21). Follow the leader(ship) spending. *Chief Learning Officer*. https://www.chieflearningofficer.com/2018/03/21/follow-the-leadership-spending/

Pugh, M., & Broome, N. (2020). Dialogical coaching: An experiential approach to personal and professional development. *Consulting Psychology Journal, 72*(3), 223–241. https://doi.org/10.1037/cpb0000162

Rego, P., Radonsky, T., Rego, L., & Williams, P. (2015). Coaching for all: Creative leadership conversations with peers. In D. D. Riddle, E. R. Hoole, & E. C. D. Gullette (Eds.), *The Center for Creative Leadership handbook of coaching in organizations* (pp. 339–346). John Wiley & Sons. https://doi.org/10.1002/9781119207535.ch13

Riddle, D. D., Hoole, E. R., & Gullette, E. C. D. (Eds.). (2015). *The Center for Creative Leadership handbook of coaching in organizations*. John Wiley & Sons. https://doi.org/10.1002/9781119207535

Rock, D., & Page, L. (2009). *Coaching with the brain in mind*. Wiley.

Rosinski, P. (2003). Coaching across cultures. *The International Journal of Coaching in Organizations, 1*, 99–106.

Roth, A. (2017). Coaching a client with a different cultural background: Does it matter? *International Journal of Evidence Based Coaching and Mentoring, 15*, 30–43.

Rousmaniere, T., Goodyear, R. K., Miller, S. D., & Wampold, B. E. (Eds.). (2017). *The cycle of excellence: Using deliberate practice to improve supervision and training*. Wiley-Blackwell. https://doi.org/10.1002/9781119165590

Schein, E. (1999). *Process consultation revisited: Building the helping relationship*. Addison Wesley.

Scott, J. C., & Reynolds, D. H. (2010). *Handbook of workplace assessment: Evidence-based practices for selecting and developing organizational talent*. Jossey-Bass.

Sharf, R. S. (2010). *Theories of psychotherapy and counseling: Concepts and cases* (5th ed.). Brooks/Cole.

Silzer, R., Davis, S., & Vandaveer, V. (2018, April 18). *Individual leadership assessment process and development: Module 1. An overview for experienced assessors* [Paper presentation]. Society of Industrial and Organizational Psychology Annual Conference, Chicago, IL, United States.

Silzer, R., & Jeanneret, R. (2011). Individual psychological assessment: A practice and science in search of common ground. *Industrial and Organizational Psychology: Perspectives on Science and Practice, 4*(3), 270–296. https://doi.org/10.1111/j.1754-9434.2011.01341.x

Society for Industrial and Organizational Psychology. (2018). *Principles for the validation and use of personnel selection procedures* (5th ed.). American Psychological Association. https://www.apa.org/ed/accreditation/about/policies/personnel-selection-procedures.pdf

Steinbrenner, D., & Schlosser, B. (2011). The coaching impact study: A case study in successful evaluation. In G. Hernez-Broome & L. A. Boyce (Eds.), *Advancing executive coaching: Setting the course for successful leadership coaching* (pp. 369–400). Wiley.

Stevenson, H. (2004). *Paradox: A Gestalt theory of change.* https://www.clevelandconsultinggroup.com/pdfs/paradoxical_theory_of_change_iii.pdf

Stoltzfus, T. (2008). *Coaching questions: A coach's guide to powerful asking skills.* Coach22.

Stout-Rostron, S. (2014). *Business coaching international: Transforming individuals and organizations* (2nd ed.). Karnac Books.

Stout-Rostron, S., van Rensburg, M. J., & Sampaio, D. M. (2014). Diversity, culture and gender. In S. Stout-Rostron (Ed.), *Business coaching international: Transforming individuals and organizations* (2nd ed., pp. 173–232). Karnac Books.

Theeboom, T., van Vianen, A., & Beersma, B. (2013). Does coaching work? A meta-analysis on the effects of coaching on individual level outcomes in an organizational context. *Journal of Positive Psychology, 9*(1), 1–18. https://doi.org/10.1080/17439760.2013.837499

Tracey, T. J. G., Wampold, B. E., Lichtenberg, J. W., & Goodyear, R. K. (2014). Expertise in psychotherapy: An elusive goal? *American Psychologist, 69*(3), 218–229. https://doi.org/10.1037/a0035099

Turner, R. A. (2007). Culture wars in the workplace: Interpersonal subtlety, emotional expression, and the self-concept. *Consulting Psychology Journal, 59*(4), 244–253. https://doi.org/10.1037/1065-9293.59.4.244

Vandaveer, V. V. (2012a). Dyadic team development across cultures: A case study. *Consulting Psychology Journal: Practice and Research, 64,* 279–294. https://doi.org/10.1037/a0031652

Vandaveer, V. V. (2012b, December 6–7). *Self as key instrument in the executive coaching process: Assessment and improvement* [Master Class]. Annual

Conference of the British Psychological Society, Special Group in Coaching Psychology (SGCP), Birmingham, United Kingdom.

Vandaveer, V. V. (2017, September 15). *The crucial role of relationship in organizational consulting psychology: What does "excellence" look like?* [Keynote address]. Seventh International Congress of Coaching Psychology, Aalborg, Denmark.

Vandaveer, V. V. (2020, October 6–9). *Adversity, challenge and flourishing: The role of I/O in coaching psychology* [Keynote address]. Tenth International Congress of Coaching Psychology, London, England (virtual).

Vandaveer, V. V., Lowman, R. L., Pearlman, K., & Brannick, J. P. (2016). A practice analysis of coaching psychology: Toward a foundational competency model. *Consulting Psychology Journal, 68*(2), 118–142. https://doi.org/10.1037/cpb0000057

Vandaveer, V., Norton, L., & Sawhney, A. (2019, February 6–10). *Psychological assessment for selection and development of leaders: Essential skills for consulting psychologist assessors* [Workshop]. Annual Conference of the Society of Consulting Psychology, Fort Worth, TX, United States.

Vandaveer, V. V., & Palmer, S. (2016). International perspectives on becoming a master coaching psychologist. *Consulting Psychology Journal, 68*(2), 99–104. https://doi.org/10.1037/cpb0000063

Vandaveer, V., Sawhney, A., & Caruso, D. (2020, February 6–9). *Psychological assessment for selection and development of leaders: The science and art of interpretation across measures* [Workshop]. Annual Conference of the Society of Psychologists in Management and the Society of Consulting Psychology, Philadelphia, PA, United States.

Van Oosten, E. B., McBride-Walker, S. M., & Taylor, S. N. (2019). Investigating what matters: The impact of emotional and social competency development and executive coaching on leader outcomes. *Consulting Psychology Journal, 71*(4), 249–269. https://doi.org/10.1037/cpb0000141

Vygotsky, L. S. (1978). *Mind in society: The development of higher psychological processes.* Harvard University Press.

Wasylyshyn, K. M. (2003). Executive coaching: An outcome study. *Consulting Psychology Journal, 55*(2), 94–106. https://doi.org/10.1037/1061-4087.55.2.94

Wasylyshyn, K. M. (2014). *Destined to lead: Executive coaching and lessons for leadership development.* Palgrave Macmillan.

Wasylyshyn, K. M. (2015). The trusted leadership advisor: Another view from the bridge between business and psychology. *Consulting Psychology Journal, 67*(4), 279–297. https://doi.org/10.1037/cpb0000050

Wasylyshyn, K. M. (2017). From here to certainty: Becoming CEO and how a trusted leadership advisor (TLA) helped the client get there. *Consulting Psychology Journal, 69*(1), 1–25. https://doi.org/10.1037/cpb0000071

Wasylyshyn, K. M. (2019). The trusted leadership advisor: Defined, unpacked, encouraged. *Consulting Psychology Journal, 71*(1), 1–15. https://doi.org/10.1037/cpb0000126

Weiss, P. (2019). *Three levels of coaching.* https://www.newventureswest.com/three-levels-of-coaching

Welsh, D. T., Ordóñez, L. D., Snyder, D. G., & Christian, M. S. (2015). The slippery slope: How small ethical transgressions pave the way for larger future transgressions. *Journal of Applied Psychology, 100*(1), 114–127. https://doi.org/10.1037/a0036950

Westfall, C. (2019, June). Leadership development is a $366 billion industry: Here's why most programs don't work. *Forbes.* https://www.forbes.com/sites/chriswestfall/2019/06/20/leadership-development-why-most-programs-dont-work/?sh=2d9c8d5261de

White, D. (2006). *Coaching leaders.* Jossey-Bass.

Whitmore, J. (1992). *Coaching for performance: A practical guide to growing your own skills.* Nicholas Brealey.

Whitmore, J. (2017). *Coaching for performance: The principles and practice of coaching and leadership* (5th ed.). Nicholas Brealey.

Williams, J., & Lowman, R. L. (2018). The efficacy of executive coaching: An empirical investigation of two approaches using random assignment and a switching-replications design. *Consulting Psychology Journal, 70*(3), 227–249. https://doi.org/10.1037/cpb0000115

Winum, P., Nielsen, T., & Bradford, R. (2002). Assessing the impact of organizational consulting. In R. L. Lowman (Ed.), *Handbook of organizational consulting psychology: A comprehensive guide to theories, skills, and techniques* (pp. 645–667). Jossey-Bass.

Index

About the Authors

Vicki V. Vandaveer, PhD, is an independent organizational consulting and coaching psychologist based in Houston, Texas. A Fellow of the American Psychological Association (APA), Society of Consulting Psychology (SCP), Society for Industrial and Organizational Psychology (SIOP), and International Society for Coaching Psychology (ISCP), she received her PhD in industrial and organizational (I/O) psychology from the University of Houston in 1981. Dr. Vandaveer launched her consultancy in 1993 after 10 years as internal I/O psychologist with Shell and Southwestern Bell, and 2 years with Jeanneret & Associates. Since 1993 she has provided advisory consultation to organizational leaders—primarily on organizational transformation and executive coaching—including cross-culturally in 22 countries. Clients have included large international corporations, academic medical centers, professional services firms, and nonprofit organizations. Professionally, Dr. Vandaveer has written six peer-reviewed journal articles and is currently writing the chapter on executive coaching for a psychology professional practice handbook. She has served in numerous elective positions in APA, SCP, SIOP, and ISCP. Awards have included 2016 Elliott Jaques Memorial Publication Award for most outstanding article in *Consulting Psychology Journal* in 2016; SCP's RHR International Award for Excellence in Consultation (2009); an exemplary impact commendation in 2006 for leading Hurricane Katrina aid and relief efforts by I/O and consulting psychologists for New Orleans; and in 2020 recognition for the most downloaded journal article in the *Consulting Psychology Journal*, "Dyadic Team Development Across Cultures: A Case Study" (2012).

Michael H. Frisch, PhD, received his PhD in industrial/organizational psychology from Rice University and his MS from Georgia Institute of Technology. He is a member of the Society for Industrial and Organizational Psychology (SIOP) and a Fellow of both the American Psychological Association (APA) and Division 13, the Society of Consulting Psychology, of the APA. He is a licensed psychologist in New York State. His expertise covers many human resource topics, including competency models, executive development, talent planning, and performance management. Dr. Frisch's focus is on executive coaching services with clients in a wide range of industries. He also serves as a supervising coach and coaching instructor for both internal and external coaches through his affiliation with iCoachNewYork, a coach training and consulting firm. iCoachNewYork partners with the Zicklin School of Business of Baruch College to deliver a certificate program in professional coaching. Prior roles include director of coaching services for Personnel Decisions International's New York operating office and manager of management development for PepsiCo. He has presented to groups such as The Conference Board, SIOP's Leading Edge Consortium, and annual conference workshops. Dr. Frisch is the coauthor of a chapter in SIOP's *Advancing Executive Coaching: Setting the Course for Successful Leadership Coaching* (2011) and coauthor of *Becoming an Exceptional Executive Coach: Use Your Knowledge, Experience, and Intuition to Help Leaders Excel* (2012).